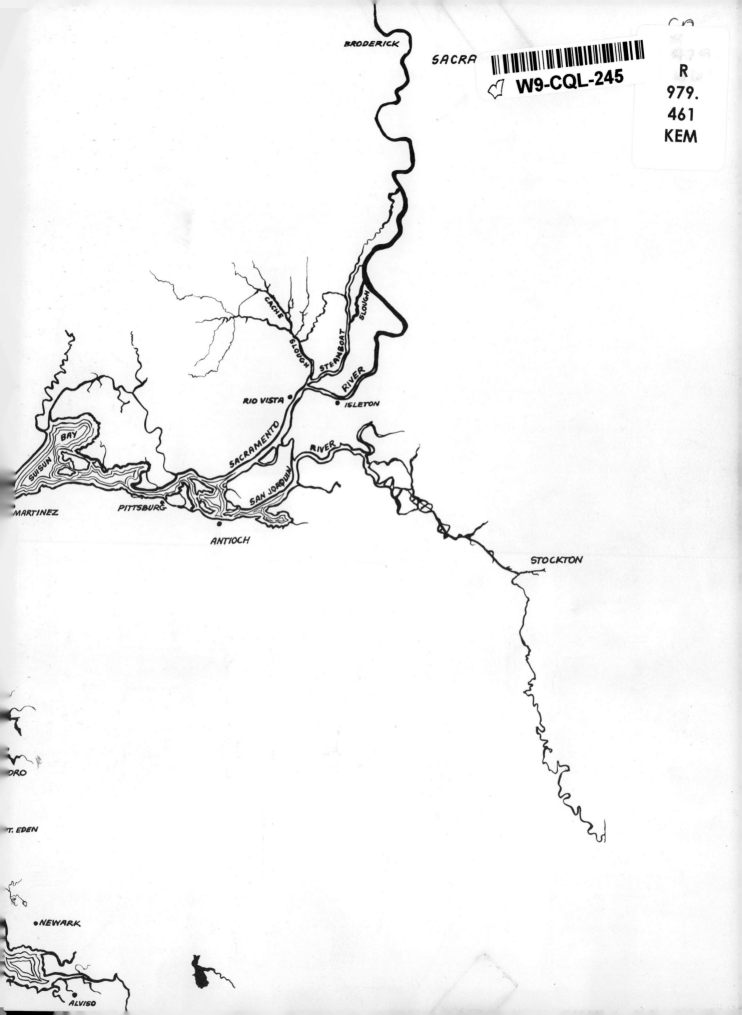

BRODERICK

SACRA

CACHE SLOUGH

STEAMBOAT SLOUGH

RIVER

RIO VISTA

ISLETON

BAY

SUISUN

SACRAMENTO RIVER

SAN JOAQUIN

MARTINEZ

PITTSBURG

ANTIOCH

STOCKTON

DRO

T. EDEN

NEWARK

ALVISO

San Francisco Bay

San

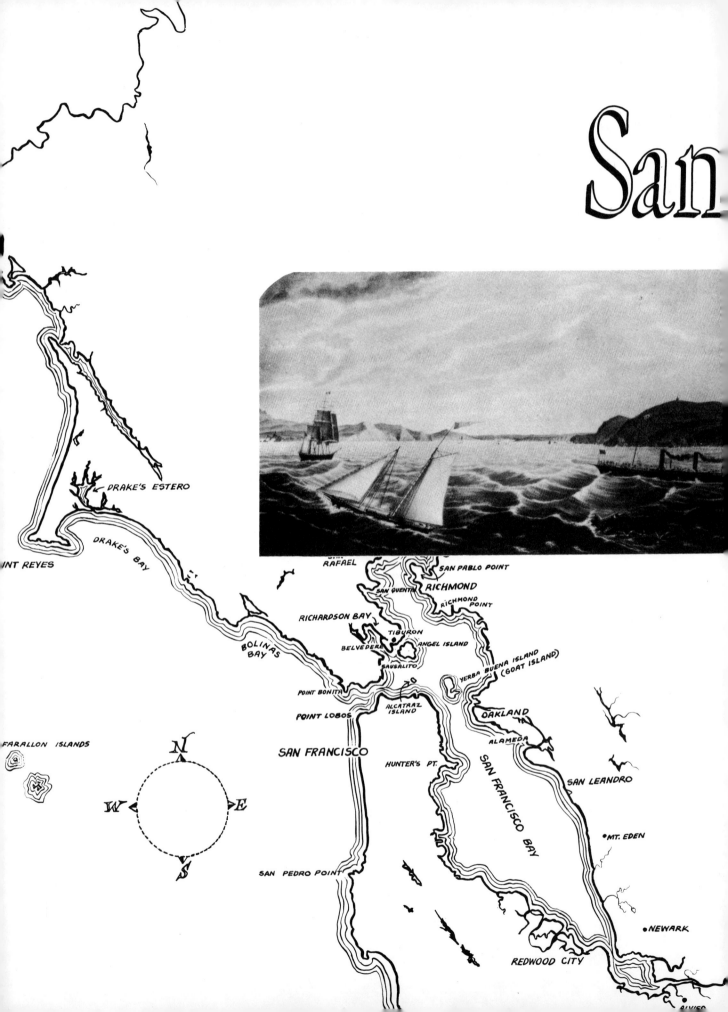

DRAKE'S ESTERO

INT REYES

DRAKE'S BAY

BOLINAS
BAY

POINT BONITA

POINT LOBOS

ALCATRAZ
ISLAND

SAN FRANCISCO

HUNTER'S PT.

FARALLON ISLANDS

SAN PEDRO POINT

N
W E
S

SAN
RAFAEL

SAN PABLO POINT

SAN QUENTIN

RICHMOND

RICHMOND
POINT

RICHARDSON BAY

TIBURON

BELVEDERE

ANGEL ISLAND

SAUSALITO

YERBA BUENA ISLAND
(GOAT ISLAND)

OAKLAND

ALAMEDA

SAN LEANDRO

SAN FRANCISCO BAY

•MT. EDEN

•NEWARK

REDWOOD CITY

ALVISO

Francisco Bay

A Pictorial Maritime History

By JOHN HASKELL KEMBLE

PROFESSOR OF HISTORY IN POMONA COLLEGE, CLAREMONT, CALIF.

BONANZA BOOKS • NEW YORK

To

IRA OSCAR KEMBLE

517016982
© MCMXLVII CORNELL MARITIME PRESS

Library of Congress Catalog Card Number 57-11362

*This edition published by Bonanza Books,
a division of Crown Publishers,
by arrangement with Cornell Maritime Press.*

(E)

Manufactured in the United States of America

Contents

I. BEFORE THE AMERICAN CONQUEST

II. THE PORT OF SAN FRANCISCO

III. MEN AND SERVICES OF THE WATERFRONT

IV. PORTS AROUND THE BAY

V. THE RIVER PORTS

VI. BUILDING AND REPAIRING SHIPS

VII. CARRIERS OF BAY AND RIVERS

VIII. BAY FISHERMEN

IX. WHALING AND DEEP-SEA FISHING

X. USEFUL CRAFT

XI. AMERICANS IN THE CAPE HORN TRADE

XII. SQUARE-RIGGERS UNDER OTHER FLAGS

XIII. SAIL IN THE PACIFIC TRADES

XIV. COASTWISE SHIPS

XV. DEEP-WATER STEAMERS

XVI. THE NAVY IN THE BAY

XVII. SPORT ON THE BAY

XVIII. CONSERVING A TRADITION

Introduction

SAN FRANCISCO BAY is the largest and most important harbor on the Pacific Coast of the United States, and it easily takes rank as one of the great ports of the world. At low tide it measures 450 square miles of water within its shore line of approximately 100 miles. San Francisco Bay proper extends nearly forty miles southeastward from the point at which the Golden Gate breaks through the Coast Range from the Pacific Ocean, and about ten miles northeast. Its maximum width is thirteen miles and it has depths up to thirty-six fathoms. At the northeast end, it joins San Pablo Bay which, in turn, is connected with Suisun Bay through Carquinez Strait. This broad, shallow body of water with flat, marshy shores receives the waters of the Sacramento and San Joaquin Rivers through the delta which forms its eastern side. Sacramento itself is about 100 miles from the Golden Gate, and Stockton, on the San Joaquin, is about seventy miles from the sea.

A bay and estuary of these magnificent proportions have attracted the attention and interest of visitors and residents alike and, over the nearly two hundred years since the Spanish discovery of the bay, an increasing number of graphic representations of it and of activities on and around it has collected. The pilot of the first Spanish ship to enter the Golden Gate in 1775 drew an excellent chart of the bay, while the earliest known picture to show the bay itself was drawn in 1806. Although for the first seventy-five years that the bay was known it was little-frequented and pictures made of it were few, the American "conquest" of California in 1846 and the beginning of the gold excitement two years later brought a rapid increase in population and commerce, and a flood of pictorial representations.

At the same time that hundreds of ships began to come through the Golden Gate, the process of making daguerrotypes and photographs had reached a stage that it was possible to record scenes and events on sensitized plates. The years in which San Francisco has been a great port have been years in which photographs were taken in increasing numbers. Thus it has been possible to illustrate this book largely with such pictures. In fact, the chief problem has been to make a satisfactory selection, since there was space for only about one-quarter of the interesting and valuable pictures available. The pages which follow contain examples of the work of many photographers, some of whom are known by name and many who are not. William Shew, whose panoramic view of the bay was made in 1853, was the first of the known group. Some of the important photographers who followed him were: Edward J. Muybridge, Carlton E. Watkins, I. W. Taber, William H. Lange, T. H. Wilton, C. Weidner, R. J. Waters, Walter A. Scott, and Morton and Co. The work of some of these men might not have survived at all, certainly not as well as it has, were it not for the activity of public and university libraries and of such collectors as Edward S. Clark, J. Porter Shaw, Roy D. Graves, Allen J. Knight, William Muir and Martin Behrman.

At the same time that the photographers were at work, artists and lithographers were depicting the bay and developments around it as they saw them. There is a wealth of material on all aspects of bay life in the lithographs and prints of the first half century after the Gold Rush. The artist can go beyond "photographic accuracy", and sometimes is able to catch the spirit of an occasion or the indefinable "feeling" of a place as the photographer cannot. For our conception of the appearance of things before 1850, we are dependent upon the work of such early visitors to the bay as Langsdorff, Choris, Vioget and Meyers. In a later era, the romantic and yet accurate paintings of Joseph Lee form a valuable record of the bay and especially of ships in the 1860's and 1870's. W. A. Coulter, first a staff artist for the San Francisco *Call* in the 'nineties and later a highly popular painter of marine subjects, made an enormous number of drawings of ships and events around the bay and became probably the best-known of the painters of maritime subjects who lived in San Francisco. Charles Robert Patterson, who knew the bay as a seaman at the end of the nineteenth century, has painted a magnificent series of meticulously accurate and yet lively and spirited portraits of clippers, downeasters and San Francisco-owned sailing vessels. There are examples of the work of these three men in the book and the list of painters could be extended if space permitted.

The assembly of materials for a pictorial history is a fascinating, pleasant and, at the same time, a baffling task. In spite of the existence of a great wealth of pictures, there is no coverage of certain important events, and some whole phases of the life of the bay seem to have gone unrecorded by paintings or photographs. As one proceeds farther into the subject, he is impressed by the number of facets of the maritime life of the region which should receive attention. It has been simply impossible to cover everything with proper emphasis and with the right pictures, but every effort has been made to bring together a well-rounded collection, and to illustrate the changing life of the bay, the ships and small craft which have frequented its waters, and the development of maritime activities around its shores.

Even a brief glance at the map in the endpapers of this book will show how closely San Francisco Bay is related to the Sacramento and San Joaquin Rivers. It would be virtually impossible to make any collection of pictures illustrating shipping on the bay without including the rivers as well. The maritime connections of Sacramento and Stockton have always been important and, to omit them from such a book as this, is unthinkable. Therefore, the reader should keep in mind the fact that the subject in hand is San Francisco Bay in the broad sense, that is, including the lower reaches of the Sacramento and San Joaquin, the Napa River and Petaluma Creek, as well as San Francisco, San Pablo, and Suisun Bays.

Acknowledgments

IT WOULD have been impossible to bring together the pictures and materials for this book without the generous and intelligent cooperation and assistance of a great many people and institutions. I wish especially to express my gratitude to Karl Kortum, Director of the San Francisco Maritime Museum. From the first time I mentioned my plans to him, he came forward with energetic and enthusiastic assistance which was invaluable. He made the rich resources of the San Francisco Maritime Museum freely available to me, provided pictures from his own collection, placed me in touch with other sources of photographs and gave me important aid in the preparation of the captions. Roy D. Graves, who owns a splendid collection of photographs of San Francisco and of rail and water transportation in the west and is an oracle of accurate and detailed information relating to these subjects, made his pictures fully accessible to me, and generously went over my photographs and captions in the interests of full and correct identification. Henry J. Rusk, artist, naval architect and marine historian, shared with me his wide knowledge of bay and river craft and patiently looked through hundreds of pictures, making valuable suggestions and saving me from serious errors.

The following individuals aided me through their expressions of sympathetic interest, their generous permission to use pictures from their collections, and the advice and information which they gave me: Marion V. Brewington, Elwin M. Eldredge, Robert B. Honeyman, Jr., Warren Howell, Harold B. Huycke, Gilbert Kneiss, Gerald MacMullen, A. F. Nelson, Andrew Nesdall, Roger R. Olmsted, Charles R. Patterson, Robert W. Parkinson, John Barr Tompkins and Robert Weinstein. I wish also to acknowledge the debt which I, and all others who work in the field of Pacific Coast maritime history, owe to John Lyman for the material which he has collected and made available through his articles in the *Marine Digest* and in his own publication, *Log Chips*. To these, and many others, I am grateful for assistance graciously rendered. This book would have been a poor thing without their aid. I, of course, assume full responsibility for omissions and errors which may be noted.

The following institutions have been particularly helpful, and I should like to acknowledge their assistance as institutions as well as the intelligent and cheerful help rendered me by members of their staffs: Archives of British Columbia, Bancroft Library, California Historical Society, Henry E. Huntington Library, Honnold Library, Library of Congress, Mariners' Museum, National Archives, New York Public Library, Peabody Museum of Salem, San Francisco *Chronicle,* San Francisco Maritime Museum, Smithsonian Institution, Society of California Pioneers and the University of Washington Library.

The sources for most of the pictures are indicated. To the individuals and organizations who have allowed me to use them, I am most grateful. Where sources are not given, the reproduction is either from a picture in my own collection or it is from a book which is rather generally available in libraries.

Work on this book has been made possible by a fellowship granted me by the John Simon Guggenheim Memorial Foundation, and has been assisted by a research grant from the Claremont Graduate School. I wish to gratefully acknowledge these grants which have been of tremendous help to me.

John Haskell Kemble

Claremont, California
17 May, 1957.

Chapter I

Before the American Conquest

SAN FRANCISCO Bay was discovered relatively late in the history of exploration. For over three-quarters of a century after it became known, it was little frequented. The remoteness of California from centers of population and the nature of its coastline go far toward explaining why the harbor was not found by Europeans earlier. Once the region was known, it offered only mild economic attractions, and therefore its settlement was negligible until the American "conquest" in 1846 and the discovery of gold in 1848.

An expedition from Mexico under Juan Rodríguez Cabrillo visited the California coast in 1542-43, Francis Drake was near San Francisco Bay in 1578, a trans-Pacific galleon was wrecked at Drake's Bay in 1595, and another exploring expedition under Sebastián Vizcaíno sailed past the Golden Gate in 1602, but there is no clear evidence that any of them entered San Francisco Bay or was aware of its existence. It was finally discovered by a land expedition under Gaspar de Portolá in 1769 when the threat of Russian expansion southward from Alaska finally stimulated the Spanish government to undertake the settlement of the region. Settlement began in 1776, but although missions flourished around the bay, white population was sparse.

The Spanish government maintained a policy of isolating its colonies from foreign contacts and, except for occasional visits by exploring parties, and a Russian effort to establish commercial relations in 1806—an effort which the Spaniards repulsed—California had almost no touch with the outside world except through the annual supply ships from San Blas, Mexico.

Despite Spanish opposition, the Russians in 1812 established a post at Fort Ross, 75 miles north of San Francisco Bay, which served as a base for sea otter hunting. As these animals were killed off, however, the Russians withdrew in 1841.

Meanwhile, Spanish rule ended about 1820, and California came under the lackadaisical control of an independent Mexico. Trade restrictions were relaxed, and commercial contacts increased. At this time, trading ships, mostly from Boston, began to frequent the California coast exchanging a wide variety of "Yankee notions" for the only portable products of the ranchos—hides and tallow. This trade, immortalized in Dana's *Two Years Before the Mast*, flourished mildly until the Mexican War. With the passing years, merchantmen came oftener to San Francisco Bay, whalers frequented Richardson Bay for wood and water, and men-of-war occasionally called. Still, the vast solitude of the bay was little disturbed until the events of 1846-48 transformed human activity there almost beyond belief.

The entrance to San Francisco bay had excellent natural camouflage . . . . Although somewhat exaggerated, this drawing made in 1849 or 1850, illustrates admirably how the islands in the bay and the hills of the *contra costa* beyond the Golden Gate masked the narrow entrance. A prudent navigator in a sailing vessel on a strange coast would stay out of the shallow bight between Point San Pedro and Point Reyes, and it is not surprising that the few sailors who explored the coast between 1542 and 1769 should have missed the entrance. Cadwalader Ringgold, *A series of charts, with sailing directions, embracing surveys of the Farallones, entrance to the Bay of San Francisco . . . .*, 4th edition, Washington, 1852, facing p. 9.

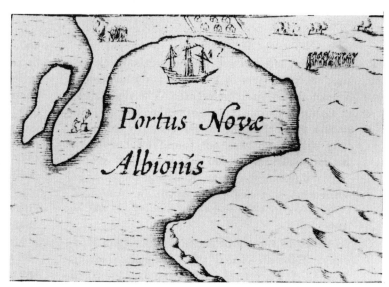

A British expedition was on the California coast in 1579 . . . . Much evidence points to Drake's Bay, about 30 miles northwest of San Francisco, as the place where Francis Drake landed and repaired *Golden Hind* after his raiding voyage along the west coasts of South America and Mexico and before returning to England westward across the Pacific and around the Cape of Good Hope. This drawing, complete with ship at anchor in the harbor, temporary fort ashore, and a visiting party of Indians, was published in Amsterdam by Jodocus Hondius about 1595. (Courtesy Drake Navigators Guild.)

Drake remained on the coast nearly six weeks . . . . This is a modern reconstruction of the way *Golden Hind* may have lain in Drake's Estero while a leak in her hull was being repaired. (Courtesy Drake Navigators' Guild.)

San Francisco Bay was finally discovered by a land expedition in 1769 . . . . A hunting party from the camp of Gaspar de Portolá chanced upon the great bay on 2 November, 1769. Two days later, Portolá and the main body of his exploring expedition overlooked the bay from the Coast Range to the westward. It is this event which is depicted in this imaginative painting by Walter Francis made in 1909. (Courtesy Bancroft Library.)

La Goleta Sonora.

Spanish ships came and went in the bay regularly after 1775 . . . . On a map of San Francisco Bay made by Father Pedro Font in 1777, he placed this sketch, labelled *"goleta* (schooner) *Sonora"* and shown off Bodega Bay which was discovered in this vessel in 1775. Father Font was no sailor or naval architect, and the sketch appears to be of a larger vessel than the 36-foot *Sonora*. It may well represent roughly *San Carlos* or one of the other supply vessels of the period. At least it has the virtue of being contemporary. (From a manuscript in the John Carter Brown Library.)

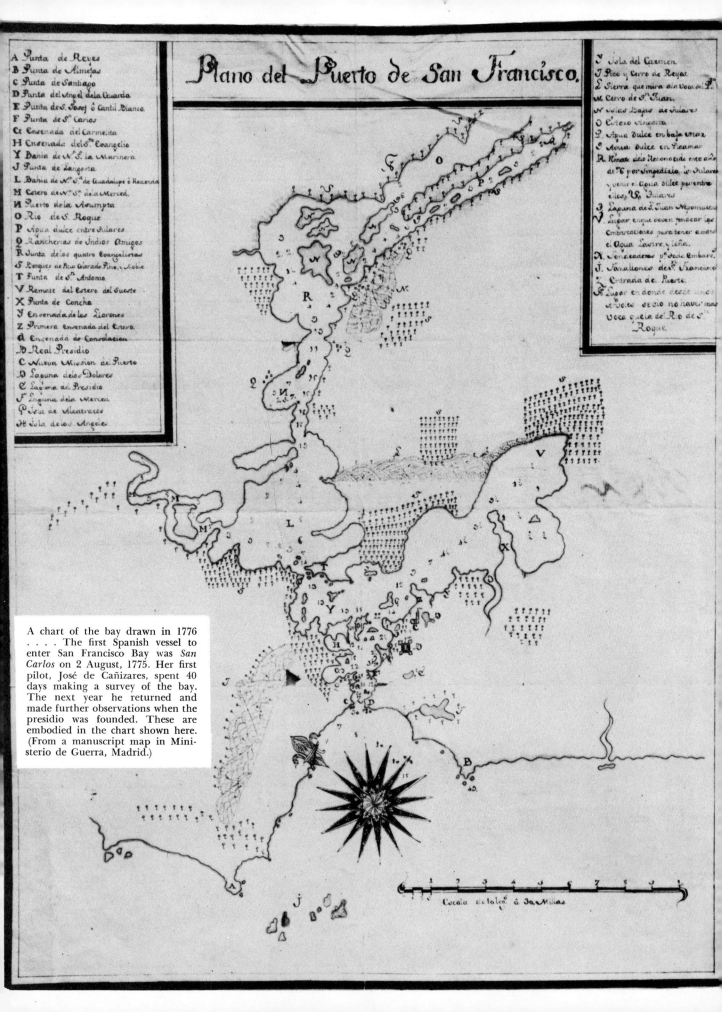

A chart of the bay drawn in 1776 . . . . The first Spanish vessel to enter San Francisco Bay was *San Carlos* on 2 August, 1775. Her first pilot, José de Cañizares, spent 40 days making a survey of the bay. The next year he returned and made further observations when the presidio was founded. These are embodied in the chart shown here. (From a manuscript map in Ministerio de Guerra, Madrid.)

A Russian party from Sitka visited San Francisco in 1806 .... Dr. Georg Heinrich Langsdorff, who accompanied the Rezanof Expedition, made this drawing showing an Indian *balsa* or raft made of tules (rushes) and propelled by double-bladed paddles. The view looks southward from approximately Alcatraz Island, and the buildings of the presidio appear in the background. (From an original drawing, courtesy Robert B. Honeyman, Jr.)

The bay was a quiet place in 1837 .... This water color, made by Jean Jacques Vioget, master of the Ecuadorean brig *Delmira,* shows the village of Yerba Buena when it consisted of two houses. The view looks westward from the vicinity of Yerba Buena Island. At the far right are two merchantmen doubtless loading hides and tallow. Vioget's brig may well be the nearer vessel. A third ship, a little to the left, is in the Golden Gate. The schooner at the extreme left has a deck load of hides, brought down from a mission or rancho landing. Other bay sloops and schooners are visible in the distance. The original water color hangs in the Wells Fargo Bank History Room in San Francisco. (From the Harry C. Peterson Collection.)

By the early 1840's, Yerba Buena began to assume the proportions of a town . . . .
This view looks eastward from the hills behind the hamlet to Yerba Buena Island
and the *contra costa*. Hide ships and coasting vessels are at anchor in the bay.
The drawing was made by Fred Henry Teschemacher who arrived in California
in 1842 and was clerk and supercargo of a Boston hide trader until 1848. Alfred
Robinson, *Life in California,* New York, 1846, facing p. 56.

Chapter II

The Port of San Francisco

ALTHOUGH handsomely endowed by nature in its general setting, the section of the bay shore which became the waterfront of the city of San Francisco underwent great changes as the result of man's activity. The first settlements on the peninsula had not been directly on the bay, but at the Presidio, overlooking the Golden Gate, and at the Mission San Francisco de Asis. In the 1830's, the principal landing became Yerba Buena Cove. Here an Englishman, William A. Richardson, who operated launches on the bay, put up a tent in 1835 and built a house two years later. The next year an American trader, Jacob P. Leese, moved there, built a house, and went into business. By 1846, the hamlet on the cove was known as Yerba Buena. It was here that a party from the sloop-of-war *Portsmouth* raised the American flag on 10 July, 1846.

Yerba Buena Cove was shallow, and at low tide, a large expanse of mud flats extended out into the bay. The physical history of the waterfront of San Francisco is largely one of filling in the cove and pushing buildings and wharves out to deep water. Before the outbreak of the gold excitement in 1848, the town council had renamed the village, San Francisco, and it soon took steps to provide for wharves to be built into the bay. The impact of the gold rush nearly depopulated the settlement for a while, and then overnight it found itself a teeming city. Wharf construction soon passed into the hands of private groups which could raise money more easily than the town government.

The State Legislature first vested power to build, regulate, and repair public wharves in the city government, but in 1863 it passed a bill establishing the Board of State Harbor Commissioners, who have since then controlled the waterfront of the City and County of San Francisco. This move was the reaction from a proposal that the desperately-needed retaining wall or "bulkhead" and new piers be built by private interests.

The board took over its duties in 1863, and between 1877 and 1914, it constructed a stone seawall along the established waterfront with finger piers pushing out into the bay from it. Between 1863 and 1955, the Board of State Harbor Commissioners spent approximately $120,000,000 for port facilities, raising the funds from port charges and the sale of bonds. By mid-twentieth century, San Francisco had a waterfront 12.4 miles in length with 18 miles of ship berthing space along 42 piers and two deep-water channels, China Basin and Islais Creek. The physical development of the port posed many problems, but they were solved remarkably well considering the natural handicaps met in the process of its growth.

7

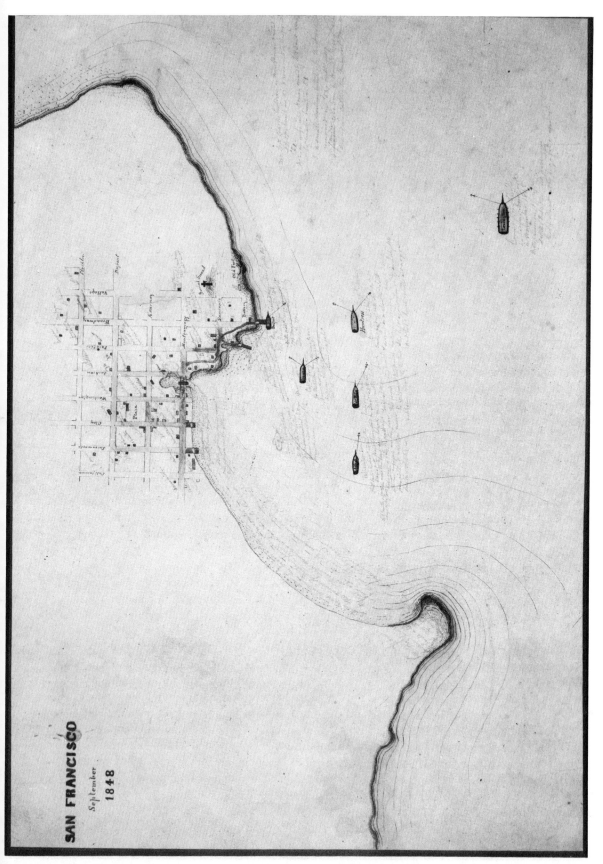

SAN FRANCISCO

September
1848

San Francisco on the eve of the Gold Rush . . . This map was drawn by Augustus Harrison, master of the brig *Belfast*, and shows the town and anchorage in September 1848, when the gold excitement was abroad in California but before the impact of gold-seekers from all parts of the world had been felt. Stubby wharves have been pushed out onto the tidal flats from Sacramento and Clay Streets, and there are two more at Clark's Point. Harrison's vessel is moored at one of these, the first seagoing craft to come alongside a wharf at San Francisco. The entrance to the shallow lagoon running inland from Montgomery Street has been bridged. Four merchantmen, a man-of-war, and a government steamer are shown at anchor. The pencil notations on the map apparently are of a later date. The original manuscript map is in the Stokes Collection, New York Public Library. (Courtesy New York Public Library.)

By 1851 San Francisco was a budding metropolis . . . . This was the official map of the city by William M. Eddy, City Surveyor. It is known as the "Red Line Map" because the sinuous dark line was printed in red and showed the shoreline as it was four years before, when the city began. The outer line was the farthest extension of filling permitted by the State Legislature which ruled on the matter in March 1851. The intervening tidal flats had already been partly filled and further work was in progress. (Courtesy Bancroft Library.)

A detailed reconstruction of the wharves and extending waterfront in 1851-1852 . . . . The shaded area indicates the section of the bay in the process of reclamation. Battery Street was built up by 1850 and Front and Davis Streets were occupied in 1851. As the shore line advanced, the wharves were pushed into deeper water. (Courtesy Bancroft Library.)

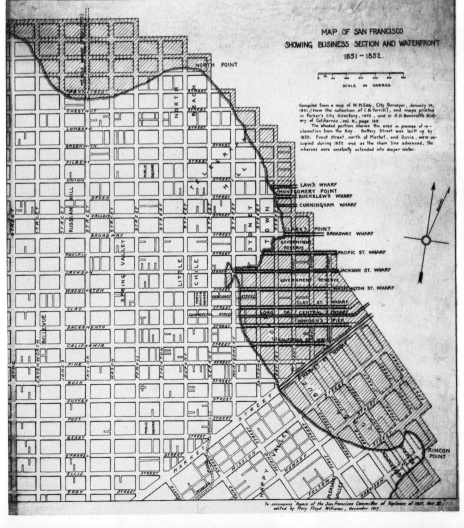

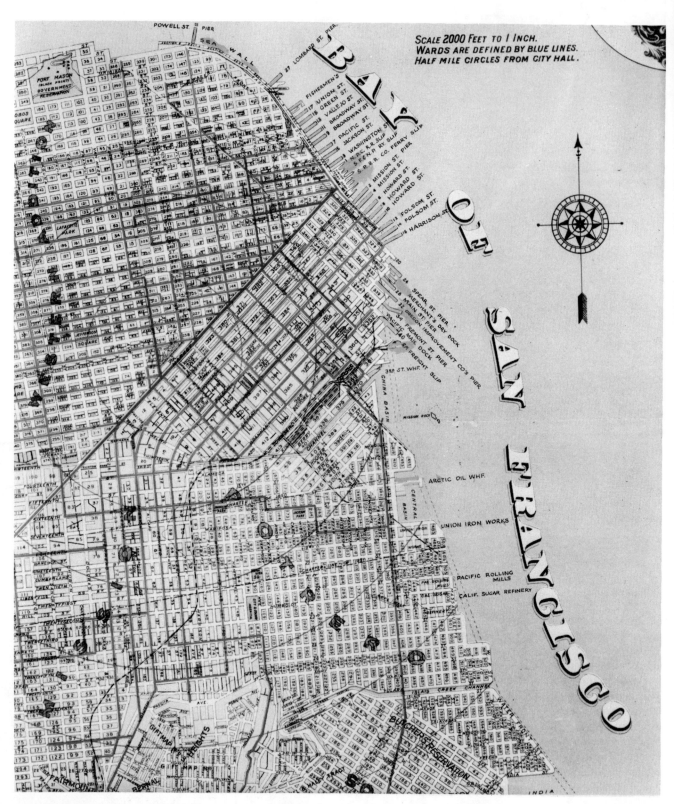

The waterfront of the 'nineties . . . . In this map of 1896, the growing regularity of the piers, coupled with the extended area of reclaimed land are in striking contrast to the situation a half century before. The seawall running as far north as the foot of Taylor Street is clearly visible. South of the Howard Street piers the waterfront still retains something of its earlier disorganized appearance. At the time this map was made, the wharves carried both the names of the streets which they extended and numbers as well. (Courtesy Bancroft Library.)

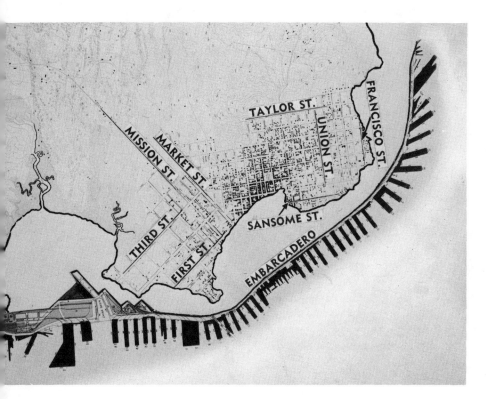

The waterfront of 1957 compared with that of 1848 . . . . The six-mile seawall underlying the Embarcadero from the vicinity of Aquatic Park at the right to the Third Street Channel at China Basin marks the San Francisco waterfront of the mid-twentieth century. All the tidal land lying behind it running back to the high water mark of 1848 has been filled with debris obtained from the hills of the city. The piers are shown jutting out into the bay from the Embarcadero with the Ferry Building in about the center. Toward the left, the largest of the piers is the Mission Rock Terminal. (Courtesy San Francisco Chronicle.)

A view of San Francisco about a year before the Gold Rush . . . . This drawing depicts Yerba Buena Cove and the town of San Francisco just after it had been taken by American forces. In the center foreground is the U. S. sloop-of-war *Portsmouth* and to the right are the merchantmen *Loo Choo, Susan Drew,* and *Thomas H. Perkins* which had been chartered by the War Department and sent to California with troops. To the left of *Portsmouth* is a coasting schooner and beyond her the hide and tallow trader *Vandalia*. William F. Swasey, who arrived in California in 1845, made this drawing which was published in San Francisco by Bosqui & Co. in 1886. (Courtesy Wells Fargo Bank History Room.)

The Telegraph was a center of great public interest . . . . The firm of Sweeny & Baugh built semaphore telegraph stations in 1849 atop the hill thereafter called Telegraph Hill, opposite the Presidio House, and at Point Lobos. When the lookout at the last of these stations sighted an incoming ship, he set the arms of his semaphore to fit a prearranged code indicating her character—ship, bark, schooner, warship, or steamer. The other stations relayed the signal, the Telegraph Hill station being visible from the city. Thus business men and others interested could prepare for the arrival of the vessel. An electric telegraph from Point Lobos to the Merchants Exchange whose proprietors were Sweeny & Baugh was opened 22 September, 1853, superseding the semaphore. Soulé, Gihon, and Nisbet, *The Annals of San Francisco,* New York, 1855, p. 465.

The Gold Rush brought a forest of masts into Yerba Buena Cove . . . . When ships carrying passengers and cargo destined for San Francisco came through the Golden Gate, they usually anchored off the town and passengers and crew headed for the diggings at the earliest opportunity. Cargo was unloaded when and if labor could be obtained. By 1851, when the pictures forming this

San Francisco's waterfront when the Gold Rush was at high tide, 1850 . . . . This view looks southward across Yerba Buena Cove from Telegraph Hill. The muddy northern end of Sansome Street appears in the right center ending in the open water of the cove. In the center of the picture are the piles of Pacific Street Wharf, then under construction. In the right distance, the hulk of the ship *Niantic* is seen moored close inshore with short Clay Street Wharf on the near side, and Long Wharf on the far side of her. *Niantic* was then being used for stores, offices, and a warehouse. Farther out along Long Wharf lies *Apollo* serving in the same capacity, and toward the end of the wharf are moored bay and river launches, a river steamboat, and an auxiliary steamer. The drawing was made by William B. McMurtrie, draftsman of the U. S. Exploring Expedition, in April 1850, and was published the next year by N. Currier. (Courtesy Robert B. Honeyman, Jr.)

panorama were taken, over 800 ships were in Yerba Buena Cove. Wharves were being built into the bay and hulks of abandoned ships served as warehouses, hotels, and prisons. The view looks east from approximately Portsmouth Plaza with Rincon Point at the right and Yerba Buena Island at the left. (Courtesy California Historical Society and San Francisco Maritime Museum.)

Waterfront activity as well as deserted ships charac-
terized San Francisco Bay in the Gold Rush . . . . This
photograph taken from Rincon Hill shows Rincon
Point at the right, Yerba Buena Island (long familiar-
ly known as Goat Island) in the center, and the ships
in Yerba Buena Cove at the left. It was taken in 1851
when the filling of land was under way as evidenced
by the pile driver at the left and the water lots staked
out at the right. Sailing vessels of all types, some at
anchor and others lying in the mud, have been de-

San Francisco in 1853 . . . . This remarkable series of
daguerrotypes forming a panorama was taken by
William Shew early in 1853. It was taken from Rincon
Point, and the inner end of Yerba Buena Cove appears
at the far left. Looking toward the right, the outlines
of Nob Hill and Russian Hill are visible, with Mount
Tamalpais on the distant horizon. Nearer the middle
of the picture, beyond the forest of masts of deserted
ships which hides the wharves, rises Telegraph Hill
with the semaphore telegraph station atop it. Next
to the right is Angel Island, then the hills of the
contra costa, and finally Yerba Buena Island at the
far right. Fences mark off water lots in the foreground.
Some of the deserted ships are in use as warehouses,

serted by their crews. These are the ordinary cargo carriers of the day, many of which were fitted to carry passengers to California. They do not include clippers, which were specialized cargo vessels with speed a prime factor in their design. Some of them, such as the

one in the left center, have been housed over to serve for storage or dwellings. A steamboat has pushed her nose up to the beach at the right. Clark Collection. (Courtesy Peabody Museum.)

and one bears a large sign saying, "Storage." There are two steamboats in the foreground and several others are moored across the cove. Although some of the sailing vessels in the right half of the picture are deserted, a number seem to be in an active status. The painted ports on many of the ships were standard on

nineteenth century merchantmen. By the time these pictures were taken, the first wave of the gold excitement had passed, and commerce in and out of San Francisco was taking on a more settled aspect than two or three years earlier. (Courtesy Smithsonian Institution.)

Market Street was well out in the bay by 1851 . . . . This view looks northward from the vicinity of First and Howard Streets. Yerba Buena Cove is in the foreground, and Market Street Wharf extends across it. Beyond are other wharves with Clark's Point on the far left and Angel Island in the distance. Many of the vessels in this picture were active in the bay and coasting trade. The forest of masts of ships anchored in the bay appears at the right. Buildings on piles on either side of Market Street Wharf are clearly visible, and two pile drivers indicate more filling and construction under way. From an original daguerrotype. (Courtesy California Historical Society.)

The waterfront was the scene of all sorts of public events . . . . This print shows the hanging of James Stuart from a cargo derrick on Market Street Wharf in June 1851. Stuart was an ex-convict who had come to California with others of his kind from Sydney, Australia. He made a notable criminal record in California and was tried and condemned to death by the First Vigilance Committee. Market Street Wharf and the other wharves to the north of it were not only landing places, but also served as business streets. In this drawing the waterfront seems quite uncluttered in comparison with the photographs of the same period. (Courtesy Henry E. Huntington Library.)

In 1853, Henry Meiggs built a wharf at North Beach . . . . Although Meiggs himself absconded from San Francisco in 1854 with city records and part of the public treasury, later to become a railroad and public utilities tycoon in Peru, the wharf which he built 1600 feet out into the bay from the foot of Mason Street remained in existence until it was enclosed by the seawall in 1881. Alcatraz Island is at the right and the Marin County shore in the distance. (Courtesy Society of California Pioneers.)

By 1855 the filling-in of Yerba Buena Cove was almost complete . . . . Dr. Fessenden Nott Otis made this drawing from Rincon Hill looking eastward. It shows how the building of planked streets on piling parallel to the shoreline imprisoned some ships. Before long sand and earth would be dumped into the water between the streets or wharves. At the far right is the United States Marine Hospital. This is a detail from a much larger lithograph. (Courtesy Robert B. Honeyman, Jr.)

The northern waterfront was still growing in 1863 . . . . In this picture taken from Telegraph Hill, the wharves from left to right are: Vallejo Street, Broadway, and Pacific. The roadway on piling in the left foreground is Front Street with cordwood piled high on it, and Whitehall boats moored alongside it as well as hanging from davits. A dredge is at work between Vallejo Street and Broadway Wharves. Two ships and two schooners lie at the former wharf, and two steamboats, the nearer being the river steamer *Chrysopolis*, are moored at the latter. At the inner end of the slip between the wharves, a ferry, possibly *Contra Costa*, can be seen peering from behind buildings. Another ship is at Pacific Wharf, while ships, schooners, and a coastwise steamer are at anchor in the bay. (Courtesy California Historical Society.)

Merchantmen unloading at Vallejo Street Wharf in 1865 . . . . The two barks at the left are ordinary cargo carriers; the taller masts and finer lines of the ship at the outer end of the wharf indicate that she is probably a clipper. On all the vessels, the lower yards have been cockbilled for handling cargo. Portable steam donkey engines stand on the wharf alongside the third and fourth vessels from the left. (Courtesy Morton-Waters, Co.)

The Pacific Mail wharf was the gateway to travel east or west .... The arrival or departure of the big wooden side wheelers of the Pacific Mail Steamship Co. at the First and Brannan Street wharf was always the signal for a crowd of hacks and drays to collect. As the signs say, ships operated both across the Pacific to Yokohama and Hong Kong and southward to Panama where they connected with others to New York. The China line was established in 1867, and this picture was probably taken soon after. (Courtesy Society of California Pioneers.)

South Beach was rather a disorderly looking place .... Sloops, schooners, and scows can be seen drawn up on "greaseways" for cleaning and repairs. The large building at the right is the United States Marine Hospital at the end of Rincon Point. Built in 1853, it later became the Sailor's Home, and drew criticism as being merely a seamen's boarding house run under a high-sounding name. At the left, the brick building is St. Mary's Hospital. The picture was taken in 1867 looking northeast from about Second and Brannan Streets. (Courtesy Bancroft Library.)

Looking north from Telegraph Hill about 1870 . . . . Angel Island appears at the left with Red Rock and the entrance to San Pablo Bay just to the right of it. The outermost building on the wharf in the center is North Point Dock Warehouse which was still in use in 1957. Just to the left of it, one of the ubiquitous pile drivers is busy on a new wharf. At anchor in the stream are a steam sloop-of-war and a merchant bark. (Courtesy Society of California Pioneers.)

The northern waterfront in 1873 . . . . This photograph was taken from Telegraph Hill looking southward. Vallejo Street Wharf is the one at the left with square riggers unloading alongside. They are American wooden downeasters since the British iron ships had not yet begun to dominate the scene at this time. The next wharf to the right is Broadway with two river steamboats (*Julia* left, *Capital* right) on the left side, another steamboat and a coasting steamer on the right side, and the ferry *Paul Pry* tucked between Vallejo Street and Broadway Wharves. Pacific Wharf is next to the right, then Jackson Street Wharf, and so on down to Market Street Wharf. (Courtesy Southern Pacific Co.)

The waterfront changed rapidly in the '70's . . . . The photograph here was taken in 1877 from Telegraph Hill from a point not far from the 1873 view but looking in a more easterly direction. The outer wharf extending parallel to the shoreline was an overwater extension of Front Street. Inside it can be seen coasting schooners and Italian fishing boats since Fishermen's Wharf was then at the foot of Union Street. Two square riggers, the one to the right with her fore and mizzen topmasts sent down, together with a coasting schooner, lie at Union Street Wharf, while the ferry steamboat *Clinton* is tied up at Green Street Wharf next to the right. Looking on toward the right come Vallejo Street Wharf, Broadway Wharf, which has been extended since 1873, Pacific Street Wharf, and Jackson Street Wharf. Goat Island and the *contra costa* are in the distance. (Courtesy Society of California Pioneers and Roy D. Graves.)

A few years brought about still further alteration in the northern waterfront . . . . The picture was taken from a point close to that of the 1877 photograph. This was made in about 1884, and looks eastward between Filbert and Greenwich Streets. What was then open water behind the outer wharves with feluccas and schooners afloat in it has now been filled. Finger piers have been pushed out into the bay, and Fishermen's Wharf is now at the foot of Filbert Street. Just to the right of the end of Yerba Buena Island the Central Pacific Oakland Pier can be dimly seen. (Courtesy Southern Pacific Co.)

Completing the seawall, 1881 . . . . The people taking their ease in the foreground are sitting on the "L" shaped end of Meiggs Wharf. In the distance a steam "dummy" with a train of dump cars and a pile driver are at work on the last section of the seawall. A scow schooner lies at anchor inside the wall, and a ship together with other craft can be seen beyond. Yerba Buena or Goat Island is behind the train at the left. (Courtesy Society of California Pioneers.)

A northward view from Telegraph Hill about 1885 . . . . The northerly end of the seawall projects from the right to the center of the picture where it meets the remains of Meiggs Wharf projecting from the left. There is a long grain warehouse on the seawall, and the masts of a full rigger alongside can be seen at the far right. A bark and a number of coasting schooners are at anchor in the stream, and two ferries from the Marin shore are heading for the San Francisco landing. In the distance, in Richardson Bay, more ships are at anchor awaiting grain cargoes. Alcatraz Island is in the right center of the picture. Taber Photograph. (Courtesy Bancroft Library.)

Broadway Wharf in the 1890's . . . . This view of a San Francisco wharf in sailing ship days was made by the Berkeley photographer Lange. It is one of the outstanding photographs of the old waterfront. A portable steam donkey engine on the wharf discharges cargo from a wooden hulled downeaster to the left. The box on wheels to the right of the donkey engine contains coal, and the barrel to the left has water for the engine's boiler. Ahead of the downeaster and also across the wharf, iron hulled British merchantmen discharge their cargoes for transport into the city by horse drawn drays. A rain storm has passed, and the vessels have shaken out their sails to dry; a sailor has tied up his shirt to dry on the forestay of the ship to the right. (Courtesy San Francisco Maritime Museum.)

The Fire of 1906 did relatively little damage to the waterfront . . . . In this photograph, looking northward from the tower of the Ferry Building, the completed seawall with East Street built over it and the finger piers extending out into the bay are clearly shown. In contrast to the ruined, burning buildings to the left, the piers were virtually intact making it possible to land food and supplies for the stricken city from across the bay or from distant ports. Refugees from the city were cared for aboard vessels in the bay, and medical stores were commandeered from the Alaska Packers ships together with sails to serve as tents ashore. The two nearest piers were used by the river steamers (*Aurora* and *Grace Barton* are beyond the second), the third by the Oceanic Steamship Co. whose *Sonoma* is shown lying alongside, and the one beyond that by the Pacific Coast Steamship Co. Still farther north is a coal pier with an overhead railway across East Street to move coal to waiting railroad cars and wagons. (Courtesy the National Archives.)

The southern waterfront when the fleet was in . . . . South of the Ferry Building, the completion of the seawall was delayed until about 1912. Looking beyond the ferry shed in this picture, the bay stern wheeler *Zinfandel* is seen tied up abaft a lumber schooner at Mission Street Wharf with other lumber schooners on the other side. The bark at the next Mission Street Wharf is probably a salmon carrier belonging to Nanek Packing Co., the Red Salmon Canning Co., or L. A. Pedersen. Beyond there are three coal piers, indicating something of the dimensions of this import to San Francisco. The stacks of two U. S. Army transports can be seen, and at the far right, the Pacific Mail piers can be identified, running out at right angles to the others. In the bay, ships of the U. S. Fleet on cruise around the world identify the year as 1908. J. Porter Shaw Collection. (Courtesy San Francisco Maritime Museum.)

25

Fashions and transportation changed, but the Pacific Mail went on . . . . This photograph shows passengers going onto the wharf of the Pacific Mail Steamship Co. in 1907. It was located at the same place as in 1870, but the surroundings have changed and the shed is new. At the left, the pilot house and stack of the company's tug *Arabs* can be seen.

East Street in 1900 . . . . Looking north toward the Ferry Building from the foot of Howard Street, the planked waterfront roadway seemed spacious and uncluttered. The bowsprits and masts of square-riggers and schooners in the coal trade and the sugar trade dominate the scene. A sign of the times, however, is the American-Hawaiian Steamship Co. sign at the right. This company was in the same trade, and shared the same pier and general agents—Williams, Dimond and Co.—as the Hawaiian Line of sailing packets. Charles B. Turrill Collection. (Courtesy Society of California Pioneers.)

Looking across the bay from the foot of Mission Street, about 1910 . . . . At the left is the Southern Pacific river steamer *Modoc*, and across from her in the slip are the lumber schooner *James S. Higgins*, the river steamer *Herald*, and a coasting schooner. In the next slip to the right are three steam schooners, *Vanguard*, *National City*, and one other, the river steamer

Valetta, with a schooner and a whaling bark for good measure. The masts of a coal ship are visible at the far right. Two Southern Pacific ferries (*Bay City* at left) and a Key Route ferry are in the bay, and the masts of square riggers are visible at Oakland Long Wharf to the left of Yerba Buena Island. (*Courtesy Society of California Pioneers.*)

In mid-Depression came the great longshoremen's strike of 1934 . . . . Although some vessels managed to remain in operation, over 60 cargo ships were laid up in the harbor when this picture was taken on 21 May, 1934. Looking east from Rincon Hill, the Matson Navigation Co. piers with their "Mission Style" facades appear at the left and center of the picture. Two freighters and the passenger steamer *City of Los Angeles* are in the berths. Three American-Hawaiian freighters and three others are anchored in the stream to save wharfage charges. (Courtesy San Francisco Chronicle.)

A liner from New York City crosses the ferry lanes, 1932 . . . . The Grace Line steamer *Santa Rosa,* engaged in the intercoastal trade, is passing the Ferry Building (built 1898) on her way to a berth on the southern waterfront. There are seven Southern Pacific and two Key Route ferries in the picture. In the center distance is Yerba Buena Island minus the San Francisco–Oakland Bay Bridge which later passed through it at the south (right) end and Treasure Island, which was filled in at the north end toward the end of the decade of the '30's. (Courtesy Morton-Waters Co.)

The great maritime strikes of 1934 and 1936 quieted the waterfront . . . . In place of the usual busy collection of trucks and vans entering and leaving the piers, this picture taken at the end of October 1936 during the longshoremen's strike shows only a few passenger automobiles outside the idle piers. (Courtesy San Francisco Chronicle.)

The bay in World War II . . . . San Francisco Bay was the major focal point on the Pacific Coast whence men, ships, and supplies went forward to the combat zone between 1941 and 1945. This photograph was taken from Belvedere Peninsula looking across to the southward toward San Francisco and the Golden Gate. It shows an LST, LCI's, PC's, tugs, and a transport at anchor in Richardson Bay. The tops of the Golden Gate Bridge towers are lost in the fog. (Courtesy San Francisco Chronicle.)

The northern waterfront in 1952 . . . . Taken from the same point on Telegraph Hill as the 1870 photograph on page 21. Angel Island is at the left, and the oil tanks of Richmond appear on the *contra costa*. In the stream a French Line freighter heads for the Golden Gate, and a Luckenbach C-3 in the intercoastal trade turns around off Pier 31. From left to right in the slips are: a Matson freighter, the Matson California-Honolulu passenger liner *Lurline* [II], a coastwise freighter, and a Victory-type freighter. In the center distance, between the trees in the center and the State Belt Line Railroad roundhouse, the roof of the warehouse shown in the 1870 picture can be seen. (Photo by Karl Kortum.)

A general view of the waterfront in the mid-'50's .... In this airplane photograph, the Mission Rock Terminal appears in the foreground. Normally it is used by the American President Lines, but when this picture was taken there was only one A.P.L. freighter alongside. In addition there is a Moore-McCormick freighter on the near side of the pier, a Navy aircraft carrier at the end, a cruiser on the near side, and three destroyers on the far side. A tender and a submarine are moored along Mission Creek in the left center of the picture. Beyond the creek, finger piers stretch out from the Embarcadero until Telegraph Hill hides them. The tower of the Ferry Building can be seen just beyond the Bay Bridge approach. In the distance, on the far shore of the bay, Sausalito, Richardson Bay, Belvedere Peninsula, Angel Island, and the approach to San Pablo Bay can be seen looking from left to right. (Courtesy American President Lines.)

An air view looking south along the waterfront, 1955 .... Although the orderly piers along the Embarcadero look quiet, six ocean-going merchantmen can be counted in the slips. A Holland-America Line steamer lies alongside Pier 45 in the left center, and beyond her is the museum ship *Balclutha*. The old Sausalito and Berkeley auto ferry slips, unused since the construction of the Bay and Golden Gate Bridges, are at the extreme right. Next to the left are the moorings of the fishing fleet with the Fishermen's Wharf restaurants about the middle of the picture. Coit Tower, on the top of Telegraph Hill, is silhouetted against the horizon, and the San Francisco-Oakland Bay Bridge is shown from the San Francisco approach to the point at which it enters the tunnel on Yerba Buena Island at the left. (Courtesy Port of San Francisco.)

Chapter III

Men and Services
of the Waterfront

THE character of San Francisco Bay changed almost overnight from that of a great, lonely inland sea to a bustling port. From 1849 onward, ships by the hundred came through the Golden Gate. More often than not, even after the high tide of the Gold Rush had passed, they lost their crews soon after dropping anchor and, in any event, they would need repairs, stores, and supplies. By one means or another these requirements were met so that the ships sailed once more, and with the passage of years satisfactory facilities developed for the manning and servicing of vessels which came into the bay.

Problems related to the supply of seamen and waterfront labor were almost chronic in San Francisco from 1849 onward. California never had any well-defined segment of its male population which turned to the sea for careers as in many European countries or in New England until the middle of the nineteenth century. On the whole, attractions ashore have always been so compelling that a maritime tradition among the people of California did not develop. Men for ships needing crews at San Francisco came mainly from the crews of other ships more recently arrived in port, with a sprinkling of local farm or city lads who found themselves at sea for one reason or another. Although not peculiar to San Francisco, the system of boarding house masters furnishing crews was characteristic there until the end of the nineteenth century.

In common with the general history of American labor, really effective organization among seafarers did not materialize until the 1930's. There had been "strikes" as early as 1850, the longshoremen made a beginning at organization in 1853, and in 1885 the Coast Seamen's Union, forerunner of the Sailors' Union of the Pacific and of the International Seamen's Union, was formed. The first serious waterfront strike took place in 1886, and was followed by others, of which those of 1891, 1901, and 1921 were most important. The shipowners and managers were generally successful in these encounters although by the 1920's the lot of the seaman was far more tolerable than it had been fifty years before. Still, a great backlog of bitterness between seamen and longshoremen on the one hand and employers on the other developed. This situation came to a crisis in the strikes of 1934 and 1936 which brought major gains for the unions which were still farther advanced by the strikes following World War II. As a result of the advantages thus gained by organized labor, the cost of shipping and the handling of cargo around San Francisco Bay increased startlingly, reducing the competitive advantage which water transportation had enjoyed. This played a great part in the decline of coastwise and intercoastal shipping as well as retarding the growth of shipping in and out of San Francisco Bay in comparison with other Pacific Coast ports.

31

The Whitehall boat was the water taxi of the nineteenth century . . . . These sturdy, handsome craft did yeoman service in transporting men to and from ships in the stream before the day of steam and gasoline launches. When a deep-water ship entered the bay, she would be besieged by ship chandlers, boarding house runners, saloon advertisers, repairmen, and the like coming alongside in Whitehall boats. William Muir Collection. (Courtesy San Francisco Maritime Museum.)

In pursuit of business, Whitehall boatmen were indefatigable . . . . Competition was often so keen that Whitehall boats were rowed outside the Golden Gate and waited for hours, sometimes all night, for arriving ships —one man rowing, one bailing. Boats carried a mast and sail which could be used on occasion. The last picture shows them on the thwarts to the left of the men; in this view the men have shipped their oars and are standing down the bay under sail. William Muir Collection. (Courtesy San Francisco Maritime Museum.)

A San Francisco boatman and his dog . . . . Robert Gibson's name appears in the San Francisco Directory as a boatman in 1874 and for some years thereafter. Previously he had been listed as a seaman. (Courtesy San Francisco Maritime Museum.)

Sons of a waterfront pioneer . . . . Tom and Dave Crowley inspect a roll of tickets for their launch service at Vallejo Street Wharf. By the time this picture was taken, about 1905, gasoline launches had replaced the Whitehall boats. Their father was known as "Hook-on Crowley" for his facility in attaching himself to inward bounders. At the left is the steel bark *Synfoed,* and on the other side of the slip is the river steamer *F. M. Smith.* William Muir Collection. (Courtesy San Francisco Maritime Museum.)

The planked sidewalk was part of the place of business of a nineteenth century ship chandler . . . . Andrew Crawford was a sailmaker in San Francisco in the 1850's, and the firm of A. Crawford & Co., ship chandlers and sail makers was doing business at 27 Market Street by 1864. This is probably the location shown in this photograph with its display of rope, cable, chain, blocks, anchors, dories, and a whaleboat. In 1892, Crawford was bought out by S. F. Weeks & Co., which subsequently became Weeks-Howe-Emerson Co. which was still doing business as ship chandlers in 1957. (Courtesy San Francisco Maritime Museum.)

A mast in the streets . . . . A sailing ship's steel lower mast is sent ashore for repair by Muir & Symon, shipsmiths. In the 1890's, young Bill Muir regularly boarded arriving sailing ships to solicit their business. Out of this grew a hobby of photographing sailing ships. Pictures from the Muir Collection appear elsewhere in this book. (Courtesy San Francisco Maritime Museum.)

Joe Harris, Seamen's Outfitter . . . . The founder of the business sits in the wagon wearing the light-colored hat. Harris did business from 1885 onward, handling slops as well as clothing. When this picture was taken, the firm was in temporary quarters at 409 Drumm Street as a result of the 1906 Fire. Next door, at 407, is John Krehmke's Young America Saloon. (Courtesy San Francisco Maritime Museum.)

Navigation schools were part of the San Francisco waterfront. Young men anxious to get on at sea patronized such schools as Taylor's Nautical School, shown here, to prepare themselves to pass examinations for mates and master's licenses. Max Lembke Collection. (Courtesy San Francisco Maritime Museum.)

Labor organization among seafarers came early in San Francisco . . . . Although not the first such move, the Coast Seamen's Union was organized in 1885, and became the direct ancestor of the Sailors' Union of the Pacific and the International Seamen's Union. This photograph shows the parade of members of the Sailors' Union of the Pacific on Labor Day 1904. Austin Tobin Collection. (Courtesy San Francisco Maritime Museum.)

The apple seller and the figurehead . . . . This picture was taken on East Street (later the Embarcadero) looking north from the foot of Howard Street toward the Ferry Building, part of whose tower is visible through the girders of an overhead coal railway. Beyond the classical figurehead of the steel ship in the foreground rise the spars of a whaler in the next slip. J. Porter Shaw Collection. (Courtesy San Francisco Maritime Museum.)

A fruit peddler on the waterfront . . . . This picture was probably taken between 1900 and 1910. In the background can be seen the timbers of one of the coal piers as well as the masts of schooners and square riggers. Notice the planking underfoot. Photograph by Isabel Porter Collins. (Courtesy San Francisco Maritime Museum.)

Chapter IV

Ports Around the Bay

SAN FRANCISCO rose to preeminence speedily as a result of the shipping boom of the Gold Rush. There was much about its location such as steep hills and wide tidal flats which seemed to militate against its becoming the great port on the bay. The presence of active, aggressive merchants and the adoption of the name of the bay for the village which had been called Yerba Buena, however, went far toward turning the flow of cargoes onto the beaches and later the wharves of San Francisco. Benicia, the early rival of San Francisco, quickly succumbed and took a minor place in the maritime history of the region.

With the passing years, however, settlements grew up around the shores of the bay. Their first maritime importance lay in the transportation of goods from their landings to and from San Francisco. Thus Oakland's situation on the *contra costa,* to the east of San Francisco, made it the terminus of the first regular trans-bay ferry. In 1869, Central Pacific Railroad touched San Francisco Bay at Oakland, and its Long Wharf not only served as the ferry landing but also for the transfer of goods from the trains to ships bound directly for ports outside the bay. In the rise of other ports, this same pattern may be observed. The passing years have witnessed the increasing coming and going of cargoes directly to ports around the bay rather than entirely passing through San Francisco.

During the era of the great grain exports from California, Martinez, Port Costa, and South Vallejo shared with San Francisco the transfer of wheat and barley from river boats, barges, and railroad cars to the holds of the square-riggers. The location of the ports on Carquinez Strait gave them a special advantage in this business.

With the twentieth century, the constellation of ports around the bay became well established. Oakland, Alameda and Richmond were the principal dry cargo ports around the bay itself, together rivalling San Francisco. Although they had earlier maritime associations, the years after 1925 saw their major growth. Redwood City was formally opened to deep-water vessels in 1937, although its traffic remained specialized in cement and gypsum. Other important shipping points for individual commodities such as bulk oil, explosives, ores, and sugar, have developed at Pinole Point, Hercules, Oleum, Selby, Crockett, Port Costa, Valona, Ozol, Martinez, Avon, Benicia, Port Chicago, and Antioch. With passing years and changing economic patterns, some minor bay ports have dwindled into insignificance whereas other landings have become active places. These changes illustrate the geographical unity of the bay and the fact that port development is possible at almost any point around it that circumstances may dictate.

The end of the Overland . . . . Transcontinental trains on the Central Pacific began bringing passengers and freight to Oakland in 1869. In order to reach deep water in the bay, Oakland Long Wharf, two miles in length, was completed in 1871. This woodcut of 1878 shows transcontinental and local passenger trains at the end of the wharf as well as deep-water square riggers discharging into gondola cars. A crowd of Chinese laborers, probably bound for a railroad work camp in the Sierra, waits for transportation in the foreground. *Frank Leslie's Illustrated Magazine*, 11 May, 1878, p. 165. (Courtesy Bancroft Library.)

Oakland Estuary was a favorite haunt of old sailing ships . . . . This picture, taken about 1910, shows vessels which were still in active service laid up for the winter. To the right are whaling ships in winter quarters. The big vessels in the left distance are mostly New England-built "downeasters" which have quit the gruelling 17,000 mile passage back and forth around Cape Horn for employment in the coal trade between British Columbia and San Francisco, the export lumber trade to Australia, and the seasonal run to the Alaska salmon canneries. (Courtesy San Francisco Maritime Museum.)

Oakland Long Wharf served deep-water and coastwise vessels until 1918 . . . .
After 1882, Oakland Long Wharf was used for freight traffic only while passengers
came and went at the new Oakland Pier terminal at the end of Oakland Mole.
Long Wharf was extended over the mud flats nearly to Goat Island (Yerba
Buena Island) to permit the berthing of deep draft vessels. In this photograph,
taken about 1905, an English four-poster, light, and with the "Red Duster"
flying from her gaff, prepares to take aboard cargo. Astern of her lies another
steel sailing ship loading for the Cape Horn route. To the left of this pair is a
four-masted schooner with a steam schooner hiding behind her. Farther to the
left lie *Melville Dollar* and one of the coastwise passenger and freight steamers of
the Alaska Pacific Steamship Co. In the background is Yerba Buena Island.
(Courtesy San Francisco Maritime Museum.)

By 1950 the denizens of Oakland Estuary had entirely changed . . . . The Port of Oakland's Grove Street Terminal is in the foreground with the Norwegian freighter *Powell River* alongside. On the far shore is Alameda with the U. S. Maritime Commission Shipyard and the Alameda Yard of Bethlehem Steel Co., Shipbuilding Division. Where the square riggers lay in the last picture are now wharves. (Courtesy Port of Oakland.)

Outer Harbor Terminal of the Port of Oakland . . . . Four deepwater freighters work cargo at the sheds, the stern of a transport appears in the upper left corner, and a tanker is moored at the oil pier in the lower right. Warehouses and the storage and distribution center of the General Petroleum Corp. may be seen above the transit sheds, and the buildings of the Oakland Army Base appear at the top of the picture. (Courtesy Port of Oakland.)

Richmond was a nascent port in 1935 . . . . When this picture was taken, the Standard Oil Co. represented the town's chief industry. Looking along the shoreline from the lower right corner, preparations to fill in tidal lands can be seen. The dredged Santa Fe Channel pushes in toward the town itself. To the left of this, Point Richmond projects into the bay with the Santa Fe and Southern Pacific-Golden Gate ferry slips at the end. From Brooks Island at the bottom of the picture, a long breakwater extends northward. Following the shoreline north from Point

Richmond, Standard Oil's Richmond Long Wharf, the San Rafael ferry slips on Castro Point, and oil loading wharves on Molate Point and Point Orient can be seen. The farthest northerly projection is Point San Pablo, and across the strait is Point San Pedro, together marking the entrance to San Pablo Bay. At the upper left corner of the picture is Point Tiburon with Corte Madera Creek and Point San Quentin to the right. (Courtesy Parr-Richmond Terminal Co.)

41

Richmond Long Wharf is the busiest pier in San Francisco Bay . . . . Some 35 million barrels of petroleum products pass over it inward and 43 million barrels outward each year. The refinery of the Standard Oil Co. of California is on Point Richmond just inland from the wharf. In this photograph, oil drums are being loaded in the foreground, and the empty tanker *W. S. Miller* is taking cargo through hoses at the right. Red Rock can be seen in the distance with the Marin Hills beyond. (Courtesy Standard Oil Co. of California.)

Richmond was a changed city after World War II . . . . This is a photograph of Santa Fe Channel in 1950. Henry J. Kaiser's Permanente Metals Corp.'s Shipyard No. 1 may be seen at the right on the far side of the channel. The former site of Shipyard No. 3 was across the arm of Lauritzen Canal to the left of Yard No. 1. Merchantmen, still equipped with guns and painted gray, are moored along Santa Fe Channel and Lauritzen Canal. (Courtesy Parr-Richmond Terminal Co.)

The Richmond-San Rafael Bridge at the time of its opening in 1956 . . . . Looking northwest, the Richmond Toll Plaza is in the foreground. The ferries, idled by the completion of the bridge, are to be seen in the center of the picture to the right of the bridge. Farther to the right is the entrance to San Pablo Bay. (Courtesy California Highways and Public Works, State Department of Public Works, Division of Highways.)

Crockett, at the western entrance to Carquinez Strait, is the great sugar port of the Bay Area . . . . The Matson C-3 type freighter *Hawaiian Wholesaler* lies alongside the bulk unloader at the California and Hawaiian Sugar Co. refinery. The small tanker *Standard Oiler* is on the outboard side of the steamer, and the hills of Solano County rise in the distance across the strait. (Courtesy Matson Lines.)

VIEW OF PROPERTY OF THE PORT COSTA WAREHOUSE AND DOCK COMPANY

The great grain docks of Carquinez Strait . . . . When the Central Pacific completed its connection through Martinez in 1879, the advantages of the deep waters of Carquinez Strait for loading grain were at once realized. Ocean-going vessels, river steamboats, and the railroad could all conveniently connect here. By 1884, grain wharves extended almost continuously along four or five miles of the strait. Half the ships clearing San Francisco with grain for foreign ports loaded at Carquinez Strait. The Port Costa Warehouse and Dock Co. had a capacity of 70,000 tons of grain and was operated by G. W. McNear and Co. These warehouses were equipped with elevated double-track railroad lines, moving-chain elevators, and could accommodate a dozen or more ships at a time. (Courtesy San Francisco Maritime Museum.)

The laid-up fleet in Suisun Bay, 1955 . . . . Over 300 merchantmen, mostly built during World War II, were berthed just east of Benicia. At the time this picture was taken, the U. S. Maritime Administration kept them in a state of partial readiness for return to service. In the background, the characteristic flat shores and meandering sloughs of the country north of Suisun Bay may be clearly seen. (Courtesy San Francisco Chronicle.)

South Vallejo was also an important grain loading port . . . . This photograph was taken about 1870 looking northwestward up the Napa River with the Mare Island Navy Yard on the far shore. The curve of San Pablo Bay is visible beyond the row of officers quarters with hills in the distance. A topsail schooner, which probably came in loaded with lumber, lies astern of the river steamer *Sacramento,* and a bay freight steamer is tied up alongside the grain elevator. Three schooners, one of which is loaded with lumber, are anchored in the channel. (Courtesy San Francisco Maritime Museum.)

Hospital Cove, Angel Island, 1895 . . . . In 1891, the activities of the U. S. Marine Hospital were transferred from the brick building on Rincon Point to Angel Island. Here cottage-type hospital buildings were constructed for the quarantine station and for non-contagious diseases. At anchor in the cove is the old sloop-of-war *Omaha*, which served as a quarantine hulk. (Courtesy San Francisco Maritime Museum.)

Tiburon Cove, about 1900 . . . . After the extension of the San Francisco and North Pacific Railroad to Tiburon, passengers and cargo were transferred to ferries for San Francisco here. In the photograph, the ferry *Tiburon* lies alongside the wharf at the far left, with *James M. Donahue* beyond her in the stream. Flat cars of lumber from the redwood cuttings to the north are being unloaded into scow schooners at the long pier. On the far side of the Cove is Belvedere, with the hills behind Sausalito showing beyond. (Courtesy Dr. M. M. Glazer.)

Redwood City began as a lumber port . . . . About 1850, the shipment of redwood lumber cut in the Coast Range became an important activity along the lower bay, and Redwood City's origins go back to this. This lithograph shows the yard Hanson and Ackerson which began operations about 1865. Sloops and schooners were loaded with dressed lumber and shingles and threaded their way down the meanderings of Redwood Creek to the open bay on their way to the lumber yards of San Francisco. (Courtesy Karl Kortum.)

The Port of Redwood City has been moved nearer the bay in the twentieth century . . . . With extensive dredging and filling, port facilities for Redwood City are located some distance east of the area shown in the last picture. The town itself is seen in the middle distance, and this was the lumber loading port. This picture was taken in June 1955 looking west. In the lower left is the gypsum board plant of the Kaiser Gypsum Co., and to the right of it is the Ideal Cement Co. plant. The finishing ponds of the Leslie Salt Co. are in the left center with storage and bulk loading facilities for salt at the right center. The 83-acre port area is in the center of the picture. (Courtesy Port of Redwood City.)

San Leandro Bay at low water . . . . The old wharf with a sloop and schooner moored to it, and the sailing craft anchored in the channel were characteristic of many small bay landings of the turn of the century. (Courtesy San Francisco Maritime Museum.)

Alviso Landing was the southernmost port on the bay . . . . This was once a lively port and the terminus of steamboats and schooners carrying on trade between San Francisco and San Jose. The advent of the railroad did much to dampen its prosperity, but for years it did a declining business in the export of fruit, farm products, and general merchandise. This photograph was taken in 1899, and shows a port which is certainly not flourishing but which still has some signs of life. (Courtesy Bancroft Library.)

Chapter V

The River Ports

THE Sacramento and San Joaquin Rivers are the natural highways to the Central Valley of California, and such streams as Napa River and Petaluma Creek serve the same purpose for the valleys lying north of San Francisco Bay. Hills paralleling the bay closely to the eastward, and the inadequate size of streams in the Santa Clara Valley to the south precluded water transportation inland from those parts of the great inland sea.

Before the gold rush, the Sacramento and San Joaquin had been used occasionally for transportation. Sacramento, adjacent to Sutter's Fort at the junction of the American River with the Sacramento, quickly became the landing from which miners set off for the northern "diggings", and Stockton on the San Joaquin assumed a similar position for the southern mines. Sloops, schooners, brigs, and even ships navigated the rivers as far as Sacramento and Stockton, but this was a difficult matter for sailing vessels, and steamers quickly took over the cream of the river traffic. Until the completion of rail connections between the Central Valley and San Francisco Bay in the late 'sixties, the rivers were used for passenger, express, and freight traffic insofar as possible. Even after the railroads had taken over much of the passenger business as well as high-revenue freight, the river ports continued to play an important part in the transportation of California.

After the first years of the Gold Rush, the increasing size of ships coupled with the rapid silting of the rivers due to hydraulic mining, closed the inland ports to all but local craft. In 1870, a group of Stockton and San Francisco business men formed the Stockton Ship Canal Co. which was aimed at reopening deep-water navigation to Stockton. This project was not completed, but in 1874, the Congress made the first of a long series of appropriations to deepen the channel of the San Joaquin as far as Stockton. In the years just prior to World War II, Stockton was opened to ocean-going steamers, and by 1950 it had taken its place as one of the major ports in the San Francisco Bay Area, albeit its wharves are nearly 70 miles from the Golden Gate. Plans to connect Sacramento with Suisun Bay through a dredged channel capable of handling seagoing steamers were afoot by 1916. Dredging of the river made possible limited use by ocean steamers, but major port facilities and full access had not been completed by mid-twentieth century.

North of the bay, the river ports of Napa and Petaluma played an important part in the development of the region from the middle of the nineteenth century until nearly the middle of the twentieth. Here, however, there was no possibility of direct connections by ocean-going ships, and the construction of trans-bay bridges and the increase of truck transportation went far toward the elimination of the importance of these towns as ports.

The Sacramento levee was a busy place in 1849 . . . .
In this drawing of Sacramento from the foot of J
Street by George V. Cooper, vessels are moored along
the earthen bank of the river. A ship, a schooner, a
steamer, and a topsail schooner behind the steamer,
are unloading. On the outside of the schooner is a
river sloop, seemingly loaded with barrels. At this
time the Sacramento River had not been silted up by
hydraulic mining operations, hence the deep-water
vessels which were able to come up to the "jumping
off place" for the mines. [J. M. Letts], *A pictorial
view of California,* New York, 1853, facing p. 130.

The trade to Sacramento stimulated the building of
fine steamboats . . . . From 1854 until it sold out to
the Central Pacific in 1871, the California Steam Navigation Co. dominated traffic on the Sacramento and
San Joaquin Rivers. *Chrysopolis,* built by John
North in San Francisco in 1860, was one of the finest
and fastest steamers of the company. She was credited
with a passage of 5 hours, 19 minutes from San Francisco. In this picture she is shown alongside the wharf
boat at the Sacramento levee. On the far bank, at
Broderick, a number of steamboats can be seen laid
up or under repair. This was a season of high water
since the overflow of the river shows clearly beyond
the trees of Broderick.

A somewhat idealized view of the Sacramento waterfront, 1856-1860 . . . . The artist shows a wharf boat and a landing stage which allow for the changing level of the river and make for easier cargo handling than when there was only the earthen bank. On the unconvincingly spacious and neat expanse of Front Street, drays, wagons, handsome turnouts, and individual riders do not interfere with a locomotive and train of cars of the Sacramento Valley Railroad or a company of drilling volunteers. The steamboats shown: *Young America, Queen City,* and *New World,* were all actual river traders. Lithograph published by Britton & Rey, San Francisco, n.d. (Courtesy Robert B. Honeyman, Jr.)

Rail and river transportation met at Sacramento . . . . Taken from the deck of a river packet, this photograph of 1869 shows a wharf brig lying between the steamer and the piling of the levee. The hand trucks on the deck of the brig and the "log windlass" forward on her are worthy of notice. Farther up the river lie a scow schooner and three river sloops. The timber-carrying capacity of the former has been increased by staging over the sides. On the levee are wooden cranes to facilitate the transfer of cargo from river boat to railroad cars. All the cars bear the mark of the Central Pacific. J. Porter Shaw Collection. (Courtesy San Francisco Maritime Museum.)

The quiet levee about 1890 . . . . Two upriver steamboats with spark guards on their stacks lie in the foreground, one outside a barge. Farther upriver, at the railroad bridge, are more steamboats and a big grain barge. Across at Broderick a barge is under construction as well as what seem to be two scow schooners. (Courtesy Southern Pacific Co.)

San Joaquin No. 2 comes through the bridge at Sacramento . . . . One of the big towboats which moved grain barges on the rivers has just passed the Southern Pacific's swing bridge. On her port bow stands a man with a sounding pole. In the right foreground a grain carrying steamboat is tied up at the wharf. The picture was probably taken between 1900 and 1912. (Courtesy San Francisco Maritime Museum.)

The latter days of the river packets . . . . This photograph shows the remarkable height of the wharf level at Sacramento above the river to allow for high water conditions and tidal variation. In order to make the transfer of cargo possible, a system of elevators at the doors of the warehouse has been developed. This picture was taken between 1926 and 1938 from the west bank of the river at the M Street Bridge. The texas deck and stern of either *Delta King* or *Delta Queen,* the last large river steamers to be built, projects below the piling around the bridge pier. Astern is the steamboat *Leader.* (Courtesy Southern Pacific Co.)

Stockton landing in the Gold Rush . . . . A photograph taken in 1850 by Spooner of the head of the channel looking down toward the San Joaquin River. Sloops and schooners, a steamboat, a brig, and a brigantine lie along the levee on the left side. Goods destined for the Southern Mines in sacks, barrels, and boxes are piled on the bank awaiting loading and transportation on wagons or mule back. (Courtesy Henry E. Huntington Library.)

A view down Stockton Slough in 1870 .... The tents and frame buildings of 1850 have given way to brick structures. Wharves now line the channel on both sides. At the right are the barge *Stanislaus* with a load of lumber and a sloop loading with sacked grain. On the left are two barges with more grain, and two steamboats. The farther steamboat is *Helen Hensley,* a Mississippi River type boat which plied the rivers from 1853 until 1883. (Courtesy Elwin M. Eldredge.)

As at Sacramento, rail and water transportation connected at Stockton .... At the left, the station of the Stockton & Copperopolis Railroad stands on the wharf. The barge *Kathleen* is unloading bricks and behind her are the steamboats *T. C. Walker* and *City of Stockton.* It is low water, and the scow schooner on the right is aground in the mud as she unloads coal. Beyond her are grain barges and the masts of more scow schooners. The picture was taken about 1890. J. Porter Shaw Collection. (Courtesy San Francisco Maritime Museum.)

A congregation of river steamboats at Stockton about 1920 .... Twelve steamboats are visible on the left side of the Stockton Channel at the yard of the California Transportation Co. The boats are well kept and are obviously in temporary layup; not consigned to a boneyard. At this time the river steamers still played an important part in California's transportation. On the right are the stacks of a couple of small freighters. Clark Collection. (Courtesy Peabody Museum.)

The Port of Stockton in the 1950's .... In the foreground the San Joaquin River bends into the picture in the lower right corner and out in the lower left. Stockton Slough or Channel runs from the left center into the upper right corner. It has been greatly improved through dredging, and extensive modern wharves, bulk unloading equipment, and grain elevators serve ocean-going vessels which come up to Stockton. Five such ships are in this picture. The upper end of the channel, shown in earlier photographs in this series, appears in the distance with the buildings of downtown Stockton around it. (Courtesy Port of Stockton.)

Stockton's ocean terminal is a far cry from the old levee .... The steamer *Golden Bear* of the Pacific Far East Lines loading grain in bulk at Transit Shed No. 4 about 1956. In the midst of the flat fields of the lower San Joaquin Valley, these extensive wharves for ocean steamers seem incongruous but they are highly efficient. (Courtesy Port of Stockton.)

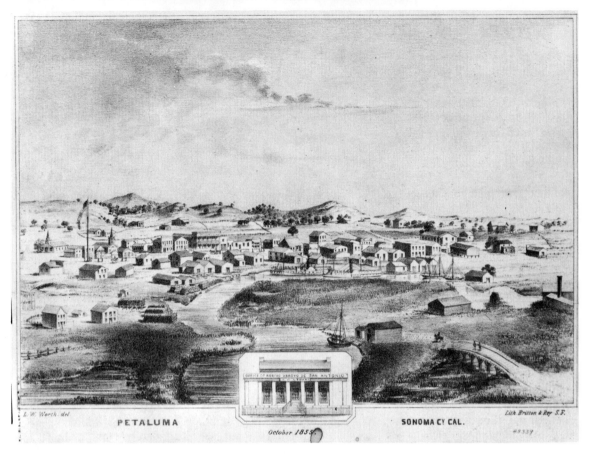

PETALUMA   SONOMA C^Y CAL.

October 1855

From an early day, Petaluma was important as a place of trans-shipment . . . .
At the head of navigation on Petaluma Creek the town began as a shipping
point, stage and freighting lines running from here to Santa Rosa, Healdsburg,
Tomales, and Sonoma. This Britton & Rey lithograph of Petaluma shows the
town in 1855, five years after it was founded. Two steamboats are shown at the
river bank in addition to a schooner and two sloops. (Courtesy Henry E. Huntington Library.)

A bend in the lower reaches of
Petaluma Creek . . . . This view of
Bodwell's Landing near Lakeville
looking northward gives an impression of the meandering tidal streams
which enter San Francisco Bay around
its shores. (Courtesy Ed Mannion.)

The head of navigation on Petaluma Creek about 1915 . . . . At the right is the schooner *Margaret C.*, a sharp-ended scow, at the feed mill. Astern of her are two more scow schooners, *Crockett* at the right loaded with hay, and *Montezuma* at the left. The barge beyond them is loaded with sacked feed, and two tugs are alongside it. (Courtesy San Francisco Maritime Museum.)

Napa River from the Third Street Bridge in the town of Napa . . . . This sluggish stream dominates the next valley east of Petaluma, and enters San Pablo Bay at Vallejo. The town of Napa stands at the head of navigation. Four scow schooners are moored at the right loading lumber. Of the nearer pair, *Plough Boy* is on the right and *Lizzie R.* on the left. *Lizzie R.* was one of the rare scows to have a full poop with quarters below with stern windows instead of the usual trunk cabin. A sloop lies against the bank at the left. (Courtesy Society of California Pioneers.)

Antioch was a favorite layup port for old ships . . . . At the mouth of the San Joaquin River, the fresh water here kept the wood of a ship's hull free from marine borers. The vessels shown here, left to right: *B. P. Cheney, Pactolus, St. Katherine,* and *Hecla,* were old downeasters which had been in the service of the Red Salmon Packing Co. and the Nanek Packing Co., rivals of the Alaska Packers Assn. They were sheathed with wood against Bering Sea ice, hence the choice of fresh water for layup. This picture was taken in the mid-1920's, and the last of these vessels was burned for her metal in 1939. Clark Collection. (Courtesy Peabody Museum.)

Four barkentines and a coal barge at Antioch . . . . From left to right, the vessels are the coal barge *Charles B. Kenny,* and the Rolph barkentines *Hesperian, Annie M. Rolph, Rolph,* and *George W. Hind.* The latter vessels were World War I-built and traded for five or six years on world routes until depression caused their layup. William Muir Collection. (Courtesy San Francisco Maritime Museum.)

Chapter VI

Building and Repairing Ships

SHIPBUILDING on San Francisco Bay began during the Spanish and Mexican periods when a launch was occasionally constructed to operate between the presidio at the Golden Gate and the missions and ranchos around the bay. The Gold Rush quickened the tempo of bay transportation, and builders at San Francisco as well as at other landings around the bay began to turn out sloops and schooners to carry cargoes and passengers up the rivers. A number of small craft, both sail and steam, came from the Atlantic Coast knocked-down aboard larger vessels, and were assembled on the shores of the bay. For the coasting trade, a good many schooners, with an occasional bark, barkentine, or brig, were built on the beaches to the north and south of the San Francisco wharves, and also at other points on the shores of the bay. The tradition of building excellent wooden sailing vessels around the bay was carried on until after World War I. There was a brisk business in building river and bay steamers at San Francisco, and to a lesser degree at Oakland, Stockton, and Vallejo. The many ships frequenting the bay stimulated shipwrights and mechanics to establish facilities capable of handling repairs as required. In 1851, the first dry dock or marine railway was completed at the foot of Second Street in San Francisco.

The building of bay and coasting vessels could be accomplished with relatively little capital outlay for permanent facilities. Larger vessels, particularly vessels with iron or steel hulls, were not built in San Francisco Bay until over forty years after the Gold Rush. In 1880, the Union Iron Works, which had been in business fabricating mining machinery since 1849, began to make definite plans to build steel ships. Five years later, in 1885, the first steel ship built on the Pacific Coast was launched from this yard. From merchant ships, the Union Iron Works went on to build monitors, cruisers, battleships, and submarines for the United States Navy as well as foreign powers. The yard was sold to the United States Shipbuilding Co. in 1902 and to the Bethlehem Steel Corp. in 1905, but for many years after it was generally known as the Union Iron Works. In World War I, steel shipbuilding vastly expanded with the yard of the Risdon Iron Works, now under Bethlehem ownership, joining Union in turning out vessels, and the yards of Moore and Scott and the United Engineering Co. also building steel ships. This building boom, however, was overtopped by World War II when, in addition to the yards at San Francisco and on the Oakland Estuary, the Kaiser shipyards at Richmond and Marinship at Sausalito built warships, dry cargo ships, and tankers by the dozen. Beside the civilian shipbuilding activities, the Navy Yard at Mare Island developed a considerable construction capability in the twentieth century.

Shipbuilding flourished along South Beach in the 1860's . . . . From Steamboat Point, which was on the location later used by the Southern Pacific Depot at Third and Townsend Streets, northeasterly to Point San Quentin and thence along South Beach to Rincon Point, shipways abounded. John G. North, a famous builder of wooden steamers and sailing vessels, had his yard at Steamboat Point until he moved south to the Potrero in 1861. This photograph, probably taken about 1860 from Point San Quentin, looks along South Beach to Rincon Point and to Yerba Buena Island in the distance. The hull of a steamboat is on the ways at the right, and a barge is under construction farther down the beach. At the far left is the United States Marine Hospital, and below it is Rincon Point Dock with sailing vessels alongside and lumber piled outside the warehouse. (Courtesy San Francisco Maritime Museum.)

San Francisco Bay's first major ship repair plant . . . . The Pacific Mail Steamship Co. began to build wharves and machine shops for the maintenance of their steamers in 1850 at Benicia. This establishment became the first large industrial enterprise in California. The plant was sold and the company ceased to use Benicia as a repair and supply base in 1868. Parts of the buildings still are in use by the Yuba Construction Co. (Courtesy Old Print Shop.)

Aquila went down with a monitor inside . . . . In November 1863, the ship *Aquila* arrived in San Francisco with an 1875-ton pre-fabricated monitor, *Camanche,* aboard. The monitor was to be reassembled by Peter Donahue's Union Iron Works so that her two 15-inch guns, mounted in a revolving turret, could defend San Francisco from a possible Confederate raider. Before the monitor could be unloaded, *Aquila* sank at her moorings. Lawsuits and salvage operations followed, this photograph showing something of the latter. *Camanche* was finally put together and launched on 14 November, 1864. She was never called on to defend the port, but lived a long and peaceful life in San Francisco Bay. (Courtesy San Francisco Maritime Museum.)

The maritime trade of San Francisco called many small shipyards into being . . . . Henry B. Tichenor & Co.'s San Francisco Dry Dock was located at the foot of Second Street. This picture was taken about 1865 and shows the brigantine *Hesperian* on the ways in the center, and a small steamer under shear legs at the left. Notice the capstan in the foreground for drawing vessels out on the marine railway. Two barks and the steamer *Hermann* are at anchor in the harbor. The latter was a twenty year-old veteran of the trans-Atlantic trade which had been brought to the Pacific in 1858 and finally went off to Japan as a coastwise steamer in 1867. (Courtesy Morton-Waters Co.)

Repair facilities sprang up everywhere for San Francisco Bay's great population of small craft .... This photograph shows "greaseways", primitive marine railways on the shore of Mission Bay. Notice the horse-operated capstan in the foreground. A dismantled steamer lies in the mud to the left of the schooner. In the distance, beyond the north shore of Mission Bay, are the wharves of San Francisco. (Courtesy Henry E. Huntington Library.)

Shipbuilding at Hunter's Point, 1866 .... A schooner under construction and one being repaired as well as a third lying in the mud at low tide are shown in this picture. This region was known as South San Francisco at the time of the picture; since then the name has been transferred to a municipality several miles farther down the bay. Long Bridge is shown traversing the shallow waters of the bay which has since been filled in to form the Potrero District. (Courtesy San Francisco Maritime Museum.)

A great stone graving dock was completed at Hunter's Point in 1868 . . . . This photograph shows the Pacific Mail Steamship Co.'s coastwise steamer *Montana* in the dock about 1870. The paddle wheels of this wooden steamer were 43 feet in diameter. Notice the wooden dry dock gate in the foreground. (Courtesy Morton-Waters Co.)

Scow schooners refitting at Hunter's Point . . . . H. P. "Pop" Anderson, a Dane by birth, established a yard at Hunter's Point in 1893, and by the time of his death in 1927 had developed a launch building and barge repair business which was the envy of other yards. The yard continued under the firm name of Anderson and Christofani. The picture shows several scow schooners drawn out on the ways together with a sloop and a launch. Another scow is afloat next to the stern wheel steamboat at the left. (Courtesy Anderson and Christofani.)

A San Francisco shipbuilder in his office . . . . John W. Dickie and his brother James came to San Francisco from Scotland in 1871, and began building wooden ships. Another brother, George W. Dickie, joined the Risdon Iron Works and in 1883 became manager of the Union Iron Works, where James also served as superintendent from 1883 to 1903. John continued to build wooden ships. Here he is seated in the temporary office of the firm on Spear Street in 1909. His son, David W. Dickie, stands behind him. David W. Dickie Collection . (Courtesy San Francisco Maritime Museum.)

The Dickie Yard at San Francisco in 1882 . . . . On the stocks in the foreground is the hull of *Newsboy,* one of the three barks built on San Francisco Bay. Beyond her, the steam whaler *Orca* is nearly ready for launching. Henry Hall visited San Francisco while making a survey of American shipbuilding for the Census Bureau about the time this picture was made. He found the Dickies to be the principal shipbuilders in the area, with a total of 20 vessels to their credit. J. Porter Shaw Collection. (Courtesy San Francisco Maritime Museum.)

Shipbuilding at North Beach . . . . The yard of Charles G. White at the foot of Mason Street, San Francisco, in 1875. J. Porter Shaw Collection. (Courtesy San Francisco Maritime Museum.)

Industrial San Francisco in the 1870's . . . . The foundries and iron works turned out steamboat engines and railway locomotives as well as mining machinery. Iron and steel shipbuilding in San Francisco developed from them. Beyond the dwellings in the foreground is a row of saloons and boarding houses typical of the waterfront district of the city. (Courtesy San Francisco Maritime Museum.)

Much wooden shipbuilding migrated to Oakland Estuary in the 1890's . . . . Alexander Hay opened a yard in San Francisco in 1868 and moved to Alameda in 1890. There he went into partnership with Elisha B. Wright. The photograph shows the yard of Hay and Wright on 4 October, 1898. At this time, the firm was credited with building more wooden steam schooners than any other shipyard on the coast. In this view looking northward towards Oakland, the vessels are, from left to right: steamers *Dora, Alliance,* and *Celia,* and schooner *Julia E. Whalen.* The two vessels at the end of the wharf and the one at the extreme right are not identified. Clark Collection. (Courtesy Peabody Museum.)

The schooner *Palawan* is launched from the W. F. Stone Shipyard, Oakland . . . . The Stone Yard was founded at Harbor View, San Francisco, in 1899 and was moved to Oakland in 1912. In the first sixteen years of its existence, it built six steamers, ten schooners, six bay freighters, and twenty-six tugs. Photograph by Walter A. Scott. (Courtesy W. F. Stone and Son.)

Four tugs under construction at the Stone Yard . . . . This photograph is outstanding for its details of wooden shipbuilding practice along the Oakland Estuary in the first part of the twentieth century. From left to right, the tugs are: *Sea Scout, Sea Ranger, Sea Monarch,* and *Sea Lion.* Photograph by Walter A. Scott. (Courtesy W. F. Stone and Son.)

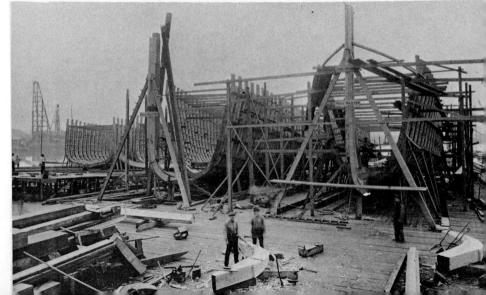

The deck of the barkentine *Koko Head* just after launching . . . . The vessel was a smart skysail-yarder built by William A. Boole at Oakland in 1902 for the Rolph fleet. Boole, a Nova Scotian, established himself as a shipwright in San Francisco in 1853, and opened his own repair shop in 1861. His yard was moved to Oakland in 1901 and was absorbed by Moore and Scott about 1908. Rolph Collection. (Courtesy San Francisco Maritime Museum.)

A four-masted coasting schooner being docked for repairs . . . . The Hanlon Dry Dock and Shipbuilding Co. was established in Oakland during the shipbuilding boom which accompanied World War I. Part of the installation was a 4,000 ton marine railway on which the schooner *R. C. Slade* is being hauled out in this picture. David W. Dickie Collection. (Courtesy San Francisco Maritime Museum.)

Elizabeth on the marine railway of Barnes and Tibbetts, Alameda . . . . This yard was established in 1914, and later became the General Engineering Co. The neat, white-painted steam schooner was built by Stone and Van Bergen in San Francisco in 1903. Until 1927, she carried lumber and passengers between Bandon, Oregon and San Francisco. She was laid up in 1939, went under Mexican ownership in 1932, and was lost off Mazatlan in 1942. (Courtesy Alvin C. Graves.)

Rugged marine engines were a specialty of boat-builders on San Francisco Bay . . . . Gasoline engines for fishing boats, tugs, and launches which met the demands of heavy duty under all conditions were developed by a number of shops in the Bay Area. This photograph shows the Atlas Gas Engine Co. on Oakland Estuary with a representative assortment of the boats into which its products went. (Courtesy San Francisco Maritime Museum.)

Benicia had a long tradition of wooden shipbuilding . . . . Vessels were being built at Benicia on Carquinez Strait in 1849, but it received its greatest fame when the yard of Matthew Turner was located there from 1883 to 1903. Turner was an Ohioan who began building wooden vessels at San Francisco in 1868 and, in thirty-three years, launched more vessels than any other individual builder in North America. Over half of these 228 launchings, which included a dozen brigantines, more than a hundred two-masted schooners, several three and four-masted schooners, four barkentines, and numbers of stern wheel steamboats, tugs, pilot boats, and yachts, were at the Benicia yard. This picture shows the barkentine *Amaranth,* built in 1901, alongside the shear hulk at Benicia. At the right, another vessel is on the stocks. Bowes and Andrews Collection. (Courtesy San Francisco Maritime Museum.)

World War I revived wooden shipbuilding at Benicia .... High wartime freight rates stimulated the building of schooners with low-powered auxiliary engines as well as out-and-out sailing schooners and barkentines all along the Pacific Coast. James Robertson activated the old Turner yard at Benicia and built two auxiliary four-masted schooners, *La Merced* and *Oronite,* the five-master *Rose Mahoney* and the barkentine *Monitor.* This photograph shows one of the four-masters freshly launched and awaiting the installation of a pair of fuel tanks which are on the wharf alongside. The old bark which Matthew Turner used as a shear hulk has sunk, the wharf has been built over it, and only the hulk's foremast is above water. In the distance, the long wharves along the south shore of Carquinez Strait are visible. (Courtesy Bancroft Library.)

Iron shipbuilding in slow motion .... After six years under reconstruction, replacing her original wooden hull with iron, the monitor *Monadnock* was launched from the yard of the Continental Iron Works, Vallejo, in 1883. The civilian contractors had been so slow that the commandant of the Mare Island Navy Yard towed the hull off across the Napa River to the yard. There she was finally completed in 1896. (U. S. Navy Official Photograph.)

The first steel steamer built on the Pacific Coast . . . . The 800-ton steam collier *Arago* was launched by the new shipbuilding plant of the Union Iron Works in April, 1885. She was designed for services between Coos Bay, Oregon and San Francisco. David W. Dickie Collection. (Courtesy San Francisco Maritime Museum.)

The Union Iron Works began to build steel ships in 1883 . . . . After a career of thirty-four years as a foundry and machine shop, Union became the first large, modern shipyard on the Pacific Coast. Its first steel steamer was delivered in 1885. This photograph shows the launching of the monitor *Monterey*, constructed for the U. S. Navy, on 28 April, 1891. There are spectators in Whitehall boats and tugs at the left and on the steamboat *Grace Barton* at the right. In the distance, a ship and one of the Southern Pacific's steam colliers are dressed with flags to celebrate the occasion. (Courtesy San Francisco Maritime Museum.)

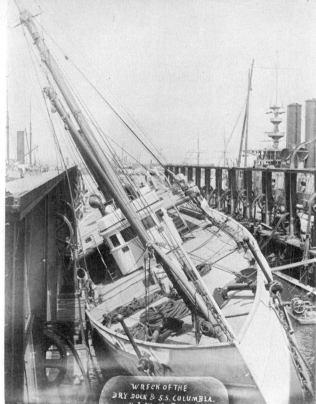

Union launches a ship for the Imperial Japanese Navy . . . . The 4,700-ton light cruiser *Chitose* was built by the Union Iron Works and launched on 22 January, 1898. Completed the next year, she mounted two 8-inch and ten 4.7-inch guns and had a speed of 22.5 knots. David W. Dickie Collection. (Courtesy San Francisco Maritime Museum.)

The 1906 Earthquake knocked *Columbia* off her blocks . . . . Almost the only damage to shipping as a result of the earthquake was this accident to the coastwise steamer *Columbia* which was on the Union Iron Works's unique hydraulic lift dock when the shocks came. She fell over on her side, as shown here, but the damage sustained was not serious. *Columbia* is also remembered as having been the first steamer fitted with Edison's incandescent lights when she came out in 1880. The camera was pointed north for this picture, and the wharves beyond Mission Creek can be seen in the distance. (Courtesy Bethlehem Steel Co., Shipbuilding Division.)

Moore and Scott's first construction job was *Edward T. Jeffrey* . . . . Long known on the coast for their repair work, Moore and Scott built this steel ferry for the Western Pacific Railroad in 1913, launching her in Oakland Estuary on 19 July. The boat had a long career under three names: *Edward T. Jeffrey*, *Feather River*, and *Sierra Nevada*. Moore and Scott enlarged their yard and engaged in larger-scale shipbuilding during the World War I building boom. David W. Dickie Collection. (Courtesy San Francisco Maritime Museum.)

Another firm which did ship repairs to large vessels was the Risdon Iron Works . . . . Like Union, it was also active in building machinery for mining and industrial use. This photograph was taken at the Risdon yard in the Potrero District of San Francisco in 1901. From left to right it shows the British ship *Dowan Hill* discharging, the bay and river steamboat *Sonoma*, the Oceanic Steamship Co.'s Honolulu steamer *Australia*, the German ship *Willie Rickmers* under repair, and the Oceanic steamer *Alameda* having new boilers installed. (Courtesy Morton-Waters Co.)

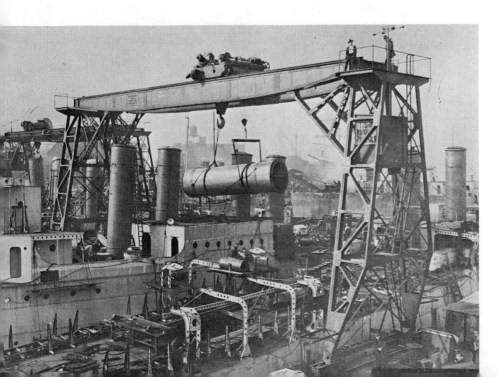

Building four-pipers in World War I . . . . The Bethlehem Steel Co. purchased the Union Iron Works in 1905, but the old name long persisted in use. In 1911, Bethlehem gained control of the Risdon Iron Works and its yard became known as the Risdon Plant, Union Iron Works. This photograph shows destroyers being fitted out at the Risdon Plant in October 1918. (Courtesy National Archives.)

A concrete ship on the Redwood City salt flats . . . . World War I witnessed several innovations in shipbuilding. The concrete steamer *Faith* was one of these. No plant was needed for her construction; merely carpenters and masons. She was launched sideways on 14 March, 1918 and towed away to the Union Iron Works to have her engines installed. Completed in May 1918, she made 11 knots on a trial trip on the bay, and went off to Chile with a cargo of lumber, carried nitrates through the Panama Canal to Cuba and sugar thence to New York. This photograph shows *Faith* before her launching, with the tidal flats of the lower bay stretching away in the distance. (Courtesy National Archives.)

Shipbuilding under pressure in World War II . . . . The photograph shows the destroyer *Strong* just launched at the Bethlehem Steel Co.'s San Francisco Plant (formerly Union Iron Works) on 23 April, 1944. As she lies waterborne off the building slip, a crane swings the keel plates of another destroyer into the berth she has just left. (Courtesy Bethlehem Steel Co., Shipbuilding Division.)

Shipbuilding on Richardson Bay . . . . On the waterfront of Sausalito, a shipyard began to take shape in 1942. By the end of 1945, Marinship Corp. had delivered 93 tankers and liberty ships for the Navy and the Maritime Commission. In the foreground are pre-fabricated parts, beyond them are building ways, and in the distance are the quiet waters of the bay where whalers and grain ships once lay at anchor. (Courtesy Kenneth K. Bechtel.)

Chapter VII

Carriers of Bay and Rivers

THE waters of San Francisco Bay and its tributary rivers serve to bind together in one sense, as they separate in another, the whole west-central region of California. Growing populations in towns around the bay and on the rivers, and the economic demands of mining and agriculture stimulated water transportation. Not until the coming of automobiles and trucks and the building of bridges at many points did the movement of people and goods by water suffer a serious decline.

The launches which brought hides and tallow from landings around the bay to Yerba Buena have already been mentioned. When Captain John A. Sutter began his agricultural development in the Sacramento Valley, he used a sailing launch to connect the fort with San Francisco Bay. In 1847, a little steamer came down from Sitka in the hold of a Russian sailing vessel, and inaugurated steam navigation on the bay and the Sacramento River. She did not last long, but was the forerunner of the great fleet of steamboats which came with the Gold Rush.

As the region attracted population and passed through stages of growth, the water transportation provided reflected the needs of the day. Fast passenger and freight service from San Francisco up the Sacramento and San Joaquin Rivers was especially in demand until the completion of rail connections between the bay and Sacramento and Stockton in 1869. Thereafter, steamboats continued to operate alone and towing barges, but bulky commodities such as grain accounted for most of the cargo, and passengers were fewer in number.

Sailing craft served the bay and the rivers well into the twentieth century. The steamers took over the large cargoes and the major runs, but the locally-developed scow schooners and sloops were cheap to operate, and remarkably handy in reaching landings on out-of-the-way creeks and sloughs. Some of these had gasoline engines installed after 1900, and continued to operate until the truck finally displaced them.

The earliest explorers of the region met problems in their attempts to get across the Golden Gate and Carquinez Strait. Ferries were the answer to such difficulties, and when population flowed into the Bay Area ferry services were quickly established. The routes from San Francisco to Oakland and Alameda and from Martinez to Benicia were the first to be opened, but long before the end of the nineteenth century there were ferry connections from San Francisco to Marin County and to Vallejo. Growing towns and cities in the twentieth century brought about the establishment of even more ferry .routes which were only abandoned with the construction of bridges.

75

The Gold Rush brought steamers from afar to the rivers of California .... Here is *Wilson G. Hunt,* a 450-ton steamer built in 1849 for the excursion trade between New York and Coney Island. She came to California in 1850 via the Strait of Magellan and enjoyed great success in the trade between San Francisco and Sacramento until 1858. After years of operation in the Pacific Northwest, she returned to San Francisco Bay, where she plied until she was scrapped in 1890. This photograph, taken in the harbor at Victoria, B. C., shows clearly the housing of her steeple engine. (Courtesy Archives of British Columbia.)

Steamboating had its hazards in California just as on the Mississippi .... Here is a vivid impression of the explosion of *Jenny Lind* on 11 April, 1853 when coming from Alviso to San Francisco. The steam pipe from her boiler gave way when she was off San Francisquito Creek and, of the 125 passengers aboard, 31 were either killed on the spot or died soon after from injuries received. From a lithograph, "Disasters of 60 Days," Britton & Rey, San Francisco. (Courtesy Henry E. Huntington Library.)

Steamboats penetrated rivers and sloughs to the limits of navigation .... This woodcut shows the sidewheeler *Rambler,* which was built in 1857, on her way from San Francisco to Petaluma. Not infrequently volunteers from among her passengers were called upon to aid the crew in pushing the boat off a mud bank on which she had stuck in the process of negotiating the hairpin turns of Petaluma Creek. *Hutchings' California Magazine,* January 1860, p. 291. (Courtesy Bancroft Library.)

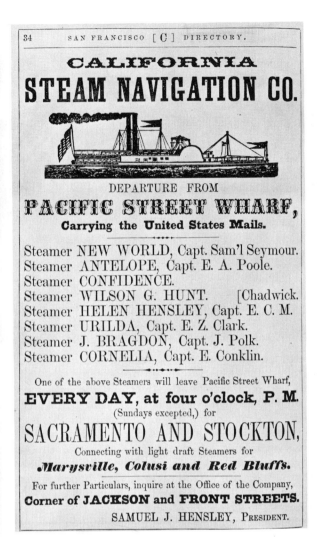

CALIFORNIA
STEAM NAVIGATION CO.

DEPARTURE FROM
PACIFIC STREET WHARF,
Carrying the United States Mails.

Steamer NEW WORLD, Capt. Sam'l Seymour.
Steamer ANTELOPE, Capt. E. A. Poole.
Steamer CONFIDENCE.
Steamer WILSON G. HUNT.   [Chadwick.
Steamer HELEN HENSLEY, Capt. E. C. M.
Steamer URILDA, Capt. E. Z. Clark.
Steamer J. BRAGDON, Capt. J. Polk.
Steamer CORNELIA, Capt. E. Conklin.

One of the above Steamers will leave Pacific Street Wharf,
EVERY DAY, at four o'clock, P. M.
(Sundays excepted,) for
SACRAMENTO AND STOCKTON,
Connecting with light draft Steamers for
Marysville, Colusi and Red Bluffs.

For further Particulars, inquire at the Office of the Company,
Corner of JACKSON and FRONT STREETS.

SAMUEL J. HENSLEY, President.

The river monopoly . . . . When the California Steam Navigation Co. was formed in 1854, it ended an era of cut-throat competition between rival steamboats. This advertisement for 1856 lists the boats and services of the company. *Colville's San Francisco Directory,* San Francisco, 1856, p. 34. (Courtesy Henry E. Huntington Library.)

Broadway Wharf at steamer time . . . . *Yosemite,* a 1,319-ton steamer built in San Francisco in 1862, has mail bags stacked on deck abaft her starboard paddle box, and is flying the "Wells Fargo" Express flag at her stern flagpole. She is about to cast off for Sacramento. At the extreme left, part of the paddle box and superstructure of the steamer *Amelia* appears and, forward of *Yosemite,* another steamer is pouring forth smoke and apparently ready to start for Stockton. A revenue cutter and a bark are anchored in the bay, and Yerba Buena Island rises in the distance. The picture was taken about 1865. (Courtesy Elwin M. Eldredge.)

Steamboats at Long Wharf . . . . On the right of the wharf, the near boat is *Antelope,* her big single stack masking the handsome eagle perched on the pilot house. Behind her is another boat with stacks on the guards, possibly *Chrysopolis.* On the left side of the wharf is *Wilson G. Hunt,* and a square-rigger is moored across the end. The men on the wharf are fishing for smelt. Photograph by Muybridge. (Courtesy Society of California Pioneers and Roy D. Graves.)

Centennial passing Telegraph Hill . . . . The railroad connected San Francisco Bay with Sacramento in 1869, and the demand for speedy boats declined. Trade from river to bay ports settled down to a long era of overnight passenger boats making "accommodation" stops at way landings with cargo figuring increasingly in importance. *Centennial* was a steamboat of this period, built appropriately enough in 1876, which plied the rivers for nearly twenty years. The picture shows her approaching her San Francisco wharf with sacked grain or rice on her foredeck and visible through the side port. In the background, the Castle, a restaurant and resort built on top of Telegraph Hill in 1882, can be seen at the right. To the left of it, and on slightly higher ground, is the time ball which was dropped at noon daily so that ships in the bay could check their chronometers. Below, on the waterfront, Fishermen's Wharf, then at the foot of Union Street, may be seen at the far left. The brick warehouse at the right was still standing in 1957, although it was no longer on the waterfront. (Courtesy Society of California Pioneers.)

The Southern Pacific named its river boats for Indian tribes . . . . This photograph shows *Modoc,* which was built in 1880, loading cantaloupes for the San Francisco market at a landing on the Sacramento River. (Courtesy San Francisco Maritime Museum).

The river boats were popular with passengers for many years . . . . Long after the trains gave faster service between Sacramento and San Francisco, the overnight boat trip was a popular one. The steamers also touched at many landings which were not to be reached otherwise until the coming of the automobile. Here are passengers on the deck of the Southern Pacific's *Navajo* (built in 1909) waiting for the boat to depart downriver from Sacramento. (Courtesy San Francisco Maritime Museum.)

In their lower reaches, the rivers are broad with expanses of flat delta on either side . . . . This picture was taken looking up the Sacramento River from a point near Rio Vista. The Sacramento itself turns sharply right at that side of the picture, Steamboat Slough enters at about the middle, and Cache Slough still farther to the left. The steamboat *Reform* is heading down for Rio Vista, a scow schooner is going up the river before the wind, and another scow is emerging from Steamboat Slough. J. Porter Shaw Collection. (Courtesy San Francisco Maritime Museum.)

The stern-wheeler *Onisbo* hauled out at Stockton . . . . To keep their extensive river fleet in repair, the California Transportation Co. operated a yard on Stockton Channel. Here is one of the company's smaller stern-wheelers on the ways. Clark Collection. (Courtesy Peabody Museum.)

The last big river boats to be built at San Francisco were *Capital City* and *Fort Sutter* . . . . In this picture, the river packet *Fort Sutter* is shown ready for launching at the yard of Schultze, Robertson and Schultze near Hunter's Point. Built in 1912, she went into the water with steam up. Two steamboats and two barges lie off the yard to join in the festivities. (Courtesy San Francisco Maritime Museum.)

A spring day on the Sacramento . . . . The steamboat *Pride of the River,* built in 1878, heads up the main channel of the river. The picture is taken from the levee which separates the river from the low-lying land of the delta at the left. (Courtesy Kenneth Clyde Jenkins.)

A bay freighter coming down from Napa . . . . One of the workhorses of the bay before she was displaced by trucks, *Napa City,* built in 1891, brought the agricultural products of her namesake to San Francisco. At the extreme right is the river freight boat *Potrero* and, in the distance beyond the Ferry Building, are the coal piers. The picture was taken about 1910. (Courtesy San Francisco Maritime Museum.)

River steamboats at their San Francisco wharves . . . . Left to right are *Isleton, Leader* and *Capt. Weber.* Yerba Buena Island forms the background. (Courtesy Southern Pacific Co.)

A bay and river freighter passing the Brothers Islands at the entrance to San Pablo Bay out of San Francisco . . . . (Courtesy Robert W. Parkinson.)

River steamers and ferries met off the waterfront . . . . The little 148-ton stern-wheeler *Herald* straightening out off her San Francisco wharf before heading across the bays for a destination in the Central Valley. At the left, making more smoke than she should, is the Southern Pacific's freight car transfer ferry *Thoroughfare,* which was pinch-hitting in the Oakland Creek service when this picture was taken and has a load of drays and wagons aboard. (Courtesy Randolph Brandt.)

Local steamers made the bay a lively place . . . . Here is the old ferry *Tamalpais,* ex *Petaluma,* steaming in from Sausalito under a plume of black, coal smoke. At the left, the steamboat *Mary Garrett* swings out from her pier preparatory to starting up-river. The date of the picture is 1888. (Courtesy San Francisco Chronicle.)

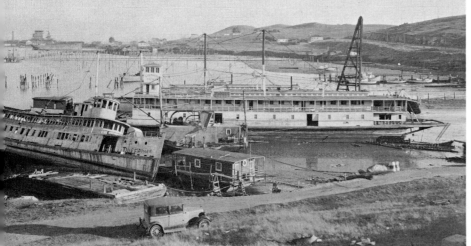

The twilight of the river boats . . . . This photograph was taken near "Butchertown" in 1928 showing the hulk of *Arrow,* formerly of the Monticello Steamship Co.'s Vallejo route, on the left in ruinous condition, and beyond her the Southern Pacific river steamers *Apache* and *Modoc* with their engines removed and their paddle wheels gone. In the foreground is a houseboat, and there are fishing craft alongside the pier at the right. In the distance can be seen the hulk of a steamer and, beyond it, the silhouette of the aircraft carrier *Lexington* or *Saratoga* rises from Hunter's Point Dry Dock. (Courtesy Southern Pacific Co.)

The scow sloop *D. N. Darlington* . . . . A pen sketch by W. A. Coulter for the San Francisco *Call.* From the appearance of the scow's rigging, she has been in some trouble, and Coulter's title reads: "The old belligerent scow 'Darlington' disabled but hunting more trouble." She was built in 1900 and measured 20.80 tons gross. (Courtesy Gerald Mac-Mullen.)

A scow schooner with a load of hay . . . . One of the most interesting of the San Francisco Bay types was the scow schooner. These were extremely useful craft, and carried a vast variety of cargoes. Here is *Albertine,* a 50-ton scow built in 1884 at Hunter's Point by J. S. Nichols, beating down Suisun Bay in the vicinity of Bay Point. The steersman stands on a "pulpit" in the stern in order to see ahead over the deck load of hay. Clark Collection. (Courtesy Peabody Museum.)

A scow schooner unloading grain from up river . . . . Serving somewhat the same function as the truck of the middle twentieth century, the scow schooner brought grain as well as hay and other farm products in comparatively small lots and from otherwise inaccessible places. There were over 200 of them operating on the bay in 1900. The schooner *Wavelet,* built in 1878 by John J. Dirks, was 57 feet long, 20 feet wide, and 4.1 feet deep. A coastwise steamer is moored behind her, and Yerba Buena Island can be seen dimly in the distance. J. Porter Shaw Collection. (Courtesy San Francisco Maritime Museum.)

The end of the trip: scows unloading at the San Francisco hay wharf . . . . The hay wharf was on the Third Street Channel, and here scows from river landings and points around the bay brought their cargoes. Their shallow draft made it possible for them to load on creeks and sloughs where other craft could not penetrate. In the foreground is the scow schooner *Annie L.*, built in 1900 at Hunter's Point by Emil Munder. Berthed inside her is *Paul & Willie*, a John J. Dirks-built schooner of 1884. (Courtesy Morton-Waters Co.)

A light-draft stern-wheel bay freighter . . . . *Mount Eden* was a smart little 73-ton steamer which was built at Stockton in 1875 and saw service until 1910. The Davie Freight and Express Line was owned by John L. Davie, later mayor of Oakland, who also operated the ferry *Rosalie* in competition with the Southern Pacific. At the extreme right of the picture is the tug *Water Nymph*. At the pier ahead of *Mount Eden* lies the coastwise steamer *Pomona* of the Pacific Coast Steamship Co. with a man overside painting and mattresses being aired. She is perhaps just in from her regular run to Eureka. This picture was taken in 1898. J. Porter Shaw Collection. (Courtesy San Francisco Maritime Museum.)

Jessie Matsen was something of an ugly-duckling . . . . A 32-ton bay freighter built in San Francisco in 1893 which, by the time this picture was taken, had acquired the pilot house of the Santa Fe ferry *San Pablo* which was quite out of proportion to the rest of the vessel, she was one of many small cargo carriers which found a living carrying goods between bay and river ports before the advent of the bridges and omnipresent trucks. (Courtesy Roy D. Graves.)

Latter-day diesel powered freighters were sometimes called "jitneys" . . . . These were often unlovely craft, but they carried a great deal of tonnage on the bay and rivers. This picture was taken at Stockton in 1940, and shows, right to left, *Eight Brothers, Service,* and an unidentified freighter. (Courtesy Allen J. Knight.)

A harbor excursion in the 1920's ....*Crowley No. 17* and *Crowley No. 18*, were 38-ton passenger launches built in 1915 for service at the Panama Pacific International Exposition. Here one of them packs 'em aboard while crowds still wait outside the barrier. The occasion is probably the arrival of the United States Fleet. In 1957 both boats were still in service, having been rebuilt as tugs. Crowley Collection. (Courtesy San Francisco Maritime Museum.)

After World War II, sightseeing cruises on San Francisco Bay were operated on a regular basis .... The steamer *General Frank M. Coxe* is seen embarking tourists for an afternoon's trip. The hills of Marin County are in the distance. (Courtesy San Francisco Chronicle.)

The dredge *Alameda* on the Sacramento River during the flood of the winter of 1955 . . . . (Courtesy San Francisco Chronicle.)

The first transbay ferries were "single-enders" . . . . *Contra Costa* was built at San Francisco in 1857 by John G. North and entered the service to Oakland that year. This picture must have been taken after 1866, because *Capital*, the San Francisco-Sacramento boat shown at the left, was not built until then. J. Porter Shaw Collection. (Courtesy San Francisco Maritime Museum.)

Alameda Point, on the south side of Oakland Creek, became a ferry terminus in 1864 . . . . In the pastoral setting of the *contra costa* of the 'sixties, Joseph Lee painted with photographic detail and accuracy the ferry wharf of the San Francisco and Alameda Railroad Co. with a train heading out for the ferry house and a boat coming in from San Francisco. Lee was one of San Francisco's first marine painters, working mainly in the 'sixties and 'seventies. Little is known of his life, but he produced a remarkable series of portraits of vessels, as well as this charming landscape. (Courtesy M. H. de Young Memorial Museum.)

The first San Francisco Ferry Building . . . . Slips for ferries were built by the Board of State Harbor Commissioners at the foot of Market Street in 1875, and the Central Pacific Railroad constructed a frame passenger station adjacent. This replaced the Davis Street Wharf as the landing for the transbay ferries. *Frank Leslie's Illustrated Magazine*, 11 May, 1878. (Courtesy Bancroft Library.)

Building a ferry slip at the foot of Second Street, San Francisco .... Alongside the new slip is the double-ended ferry *Alameda*, built in 1866 and the prototype of bay ferries for over a half century to come. At the shipyard in the foreground, a small steamer has been cut in two and is being lengthened. Notice the steam box for shaping timbers near the camera on the right. A port-painted British ship discharges at the right, and beyond her lie two revenue cutters. Offshore, the razee frigate *Independence* lies moored as a schoolship. She was stationed at San Francisco in this capacity from 1867 to 1869, thus establishing the date of the picture. In the distance is Mission Rock, later covered by a huge freight terminal. (Courtesy Society of California Pioneers.)

Newark was the biggest ferry on the bay in 1877 . . . . Built by the South Pacific Coast Railroad, she was intended for the service from San Francisco to Alameda. Her 42-foot paddle wheels were surpassed in diameter only by those of ocean steamers. Later she passed under Southern Pacific ownership, was rebuilt as *Sacramento* in 1923, and continued in service until 1955. This picture was taken in March, 1899. It shows a three-masted British grain ship at anchor at the left, and the masts of another square-rigger peering above the paddle box and walking beam of *Newark*. Clark Collection. (Courtesy Peabody Museum.)

The crew of *Bay City* . . . . This South Pacific Coast ferry went into service in 1878, later passed to the Southern Pacific, and was dismantled in 1930. The picture was taken when she was operating for the Southern Pacific. In addition to deck officers, deck hands, and black gang, there are baggage handlers, cooks, waiters, a bootblack, and a stewardess. The captain gives every evidence of being proud of his boat and of his crew. (Courtesy San Francisco Maritime Museum.)

Two famous boats off the Ferry Terminal at San Francisco . . . At the left is the single-ended ferry steamer *San Rafael*, built in New York for the North Pacific Coast Railroad in 1877, and shipped in sections to San Francisco to be re-assembled. She operated to Sausalito and Point San Quentin until she was lost in collision with *Sausalito* in 1901. The other ferry shown, *Amador*, was rebuilt from a single-ended river boat in 1878 and remained in ferry service for the Southern Pacific until 1904. A tug is visible immediately to the right of *San Rafael*, and next to the right is one of the Pacific Mail liners coming in. A revenue cutter is at anchor to the right of *Amador*, and at least four square-riggers are shown. (Courtesy San Francisco Maritime Museum.)

The second *Alameda* passing under the Bay Bridge . . . . *Alameda* and *Santa Clara* were built by the Southern Pacific in 1913. Their two stacks placed athwartships made them distinctive among bay passenger ferries and they had separate double compound engines for each paddle wheel. *Alameda* had a seating capacity of 1,879. J. Porter Shaw Collection. (Courtesy San Francisco Maritime Museum.)

The Key Route Pier at Oakland . . . . From 1903 until 1939, the Key Route was the Southern Pacific's great rival for transbay passengers. Its mole and overwater trestle extended farther into the bay than Oakland Pier, and these were eventually incorporated into the eastern approach of the Bay Bridge. This photograph of the line's eastbay terminal was taken between 1907 and 1919, and shows one boat, perhaps *Fernwood*, leaving the slip and three boats tied up. The first and second from the right are *San Jose* and *Yerba Buena* [I]. At the right, the electric trains which carried passengers to and from the ferries can be seen. The Key Route's boats were painted a dark orange which made them less photogenic than the white boats of the Southern Pacific. J. Porter Shaw Collection. (Courtesy San Francisco Maritime Museum.)

Rebuilding a ferry .... In 1922, the Northwestern Pacific Railway had their 32-year old ferry *Ukiah* rebuilt at the Southern Pacific Shipyard at Oakland. She emerged from this major operation as *Eureka,* with a seating capacity of 2,300 which made her the largest passenger ferry in the world. The photograph, taken during the reconstruction, shows the walking beam mounted on its "A" frame with the piston emerging from the 65-inch cylinder at the right and the crank connected with the paddle-wheel shaft at the left. The ferry *Garden City* is at the next pier and, across the channel, can be seen the Alameda Mole with its tracks and catenary for electric trains leading out of the ferry slip at the end. *Eureka* came under Southern Pacific ownership in 1941 and was transferred from the Sausalito to the Oakland Pier run. M. F. Silverthorn Photo. (Reproduced in *Of Walking Beams and Paddle Wheels.)*

Eureka was the last of the walking beam ferries .... Not only did her retirement by the Southern Pacific in 1956 end the use of paddlers on San Francisco Bay, but she was the last vessel with this type of propulsion in active service in the United States. The picture shows her entering the slip at the San Francisco Ferry Building in July, 1953 with an unusually large crowd of commuters aboard because of a strike on the Key System's transbay electric trains. After she was retired from service, the Southern Pacific presented her to the San Francisco Maritime Museum, and, in 1957, there were plans actively afoot for her preservation by the State of California. (Courtesy San Francisco Chronicle.)

The ferry landing at Sausalito in 1894 .... In the slip at the left is *San Rafael,* and at the right is *Tamalpais,* formerly *Petaluma,* which was built in 1857 and remained in service until the year this picture was taken. A train of the North Pacific Coast Railroad stands on the wharf awaiting the arrival of another ferry. Two British grain ships are at anchor in Richardson Bay. The entrance to Raccoon Strait between Belvedere Peninsula and Angel Island can be seen to the right of the farther vessel. (Courtesy Southern Pacific Co.)

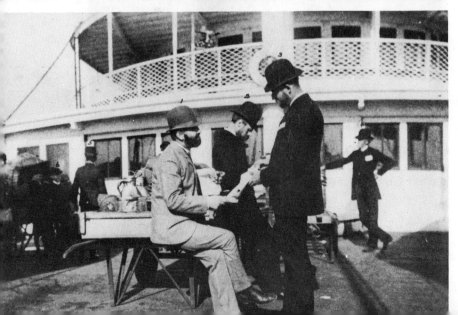

Commuters on the morning's run from Sausalito .... Passengers on the foredeck of *San Rafael* as she crosses to San Francisco. The bearded man in the light suit has his *Chronicle* under his arm, and the baggage truck on which he sits is piled with mail bags and milk cans. There is more mail and baggage on the trucks at the left. (Courtesy Roy D. Graves.)

The "single-ender" *James M. Donahue,* built for the San Francisco and North Pacific Railroad in 1875 .... She first ran from San Francisco to Donahue Landing on Petaluma Creek, which was the southernly terminus of the railroad, but in 1884, the railroad was completed to Tiburon, and she made this her northern port. She came under Northewestern Pacific ownership in 1907 and was retired two years later. Here she is passing around Alcatraz Island bound from Tiburon to San Francisco. (Courtesy Roy D. Graves.)

Ferries came in all sizes .... The little 135-foot *Ellen* was built in 1883. She was long on the Vallejo-Mare Island run, and she inaugurated the Richmond-San Rafael ferry in 1915. (Courtesy Roy D. Graves.)

Solano was one of the wonders of the age . . . . She was built by the Central Pacific in 1879 to carry trains across Carquinez Strait from Benicia to Port Costa. There were four railroad tracks laid on her deck, and she could carry two complete passenger trains or one freight train at a time, complete with road engines and a switch engine. Here she is shown at Port Costa with the switch engine pushing a passenger train off. She remained in service for over half a century, shuttling back and forth, her paddle wheels operated by separate walking beams, until the completion of the railroad bridge across the strait. Clark Collection. (Courtesy Peabody Museum.)

The Sacramento Northern Railway's car-ferry Ramon . . . . Built in 1914 at Pittsburg and powered by gasoline engines, *Ramon* carried trains across the upper end of Suisun Bay from Mallard to Chipps. (Courtesy Robert W. Parkinson.)

The longest ferry run was from San Francisco to Vallejo . . . . For this service, the Monticello Steamship Co. purchased the steamer *Florida* from the Old Bay Line of Baltimore in 1924. She was brought to San Francisco and renamed *Calistoga* in honor of the thermal resort in the upper Napa Valley. This picture shows her running trials off San Francisco after her bow had been cut away to permit loading and unloading of automobiles at both ends. (Courtesy Bethlehem Steel Co., Shipbuilding Division.)

During the 1920's, the ferries met increasing demand for the transportation of automobiles . . . . The construction of boats designed solely for transporting motor vehicles, and the establishment of landings where they could be handled efficiently were characteristics of this period. Here is the Hyde Street landing in 1931, where two slips were devoted to Sausalito traffic and two to Berkeley. Oakland, Alameda, and Richmond auto ferries ran from the south end of the Ferry Building. The rival Southern Pacific and Golden Gate Ferry Co. auto ferry services had been amalgamated in 1929 as the Southern Pacific Golden Gate Ferries Ltd. At the far left is one of the diesel ferries built by the Southern Pacific and Northwestern Pacific in 1927, and to her right is *Yosemite* of 1923. In the background, from left to right, are Sausalito, Richardson Bay, the Belvedere Peninsula, Angel Island, and Alcatraz Island. (Courtesy Southern Pacific Co.)

In the delta and river country, ferries operate where traffic does not justify the expense of bridge construction . . . . The Elk Horn Ferry, about 12 miles above Sacramento, is run by the State Highway Department and is typical of many others. A steel cable is laid across the river, normally lying on the bottom. It is brought up over the end of the ferry, is guided around sheaves which are turned by a 25 horsepower gasoline engine, and is paid out again over the other end. The wrapping effect around the sheaves pulls the boat across the river. On the upstream side is another cable which helps to give direction and takes the strain off the towing cable. Other ferries swing themselves across with a long cable anchored three or four hundred feet upstream, the current providing the power. This picture was taken in 1954. (Courtesy San Francisco Chronicle.)

Chapter VIII

Bay Fishermen

FISHING in the bay and rivers as well as in the open sea adjacent to the Golden Gate was carried on as soon as there was a sufficient demand ashore for the fish. The growth of the city in the early 'fifties, with a population which required food but produced almost none themselves, stimulated the fisheries as well as the beginnings of agriculture in the Central Valley and cattle raising in Southern California.

In the open sea, the fishing grounds were mostly south of the Golden Gate between Pigeon Point and Monterey in depths of 15 to 60 fathoms. Italians and Dalmatians specialized in this activity, and they established a tradition which outlasted a century. Their feluccas, lateen-rigged Mediterranean-type fishing boats, were a characteristic feature of the San Francisco waterfront until after the turn of the century when they were replaced by gasoline-driven craft, although some of the hull characteristics of the earlier boats persisted. In addition to these hand-liners, there was also a considerable trawling fleet, mainly taking cod.

Within the bay itself, the catching of shrimp by Chinese, and to a lesser extent by Italian fishermen, began about 1865. The Chinese shrimp "fishing camps" on both the north and south shores of San Pablo Bay and at Hunter's Point were long characteristic of this operation.

Before the Sacramento and San Joaquin Rivers were clogged by gravel and silt from hydraulic mining operations, salmon in great numbers went up them to spawn. By 1857, the salmon catch on the Sacramento amounted to about 200,000 fish, and the industry employed a hundred boats, each carrying two men, as well as another hundred men ashore curing and packing the fish. The first salmon cannery opened across the river from Sacramento in 1864, and the number had increased to twenty in 1881. From 1885 onward the industry was on the decline, and the last cannery closed in 1919.

Although there were native oysters in the tidelands on the west side of the bay, it was not until after Atlantic Coast oysters were imported and planted there that the business of taking them on a large scale developed. Several groups engaged in this after 1870, finally being consolidated into the Morgan Oyster Co. which was formed in 1887 by Captain John Stillwell Morgan and four partners. The business proved to be less profitable than had been anticipated, and "camps" which had been established were abandoned or sold for other uses.

During World War I, sardine fishing off San Francisco Bay began, and this reached great proportions in the 1920's and 1930's, declining sharply after 1944. At the height of the sardine fishery, the commercial fishing fleet of San Francisco numbered 466, and that of Sacramento 257. Although this number was large, it was less than one third of the 2,453 fishing boats then operating in California waters.

Italian fishermen were established in San Francisco in the 1850's . . . . In the parade on 27 September 1858 to celebrate the laying of the Atlantic cable many trades and vocations entered floats. The Italian fishermen mounted one of their feluccas on wheels and had her drawn through the streets by four horses. Detail from a broadside published by Sterett and Butler, San Francisco. (Courtesy Henry E. Huntington Library.)

Two types of Bay fishing craft . . . . A lateen-rigged Italian fishing boat, or "felucca," coming into North Beach under sail and oars in a nearly dead calm and against the tide. At the same time a "Columbia River fish boat" or "Columbia River salmon boat" is rowed out. This latter type was first built at Broderick across the river from Sacramento. Farther out a coasting schooner lies at anchor. In the distance the Marin County shore and Angel Island are visible. (Courtesy Henry E. Huntington Library.)

The wharf at the foot of Telegraph Hill . . . . Feluccas moored along both sides of the slip at the foot of Union Street. (Courtesy San Francisco Maritime Museum.)

Fishermen's Wharf when it was at the foot of Union Street . . . . Feluccas are moored around the wharf. One boat has her sail spread to dry. Fish nets are drying over the railing, and in the foreground are circular crab nets. A British grain ship, loaded and ready for sea, lies in the offing. (Courtesy Smithsonian Institution.)

An Italian fishing boat or felucca, moored off North Beach . . . . Alcatraz and Angel Islands can be seen in the distance. The picture was taken in 1889. (Courtesy Smithsonian Institution.)

Italian fishermen relaxing at the wharf . . . . Plumb-sterned fishing boats are moored with sails furled. Buckets, boots, nets, lines, rope, and demijohns are to be seen on the decks around the group of conversing men. (Courtesy Morton-Waters Co.)

Mending nets on the wharf at the foot of Union Street . . . . The boats are out on the wharf for painting and repairs and their underwater bodies and deep, false keels show to advantage. Masts, of course, have been unstepped. The second boat from the left bears the name board: *Solitario*. (Courtesy Smithsonian Institution.)

The "San Francisco Bay Cats" were the original crab boats of the region . . . . A fisherman boards his cat boat at the wharf. These craft, which were 15 to 18 feet in length, were intended for use inside the bay in contrast with the feluccas which fished outside the Heads. J. Porter Shaw Collection. (Courtesy San Francisco Maritime Museum.)

A large Chinese fishing junk . . . . Such craft, although designed along Oriental lines, were constructed by western shipbuilders on San Francisco Bay. Certain compromises are also apparent, such as cloth sails in place of the matting which would have been found in the Far East. J. Porter Shaw Collection. (Courtesy San Francisco Maritime Museum.)

Shrimping was a Chinese monopoly after 1871 .... Men on a bay-built Chinese shrimp boat hauling in nets in San Pablo Bay near McNear's Landing. The technique of the Chinese was to stake out nets at right angles to the tide and let the racing water fill them with shrimp. Notice the wooden rudder with diamond-shaped venting holes which could be brought out of the water. Its lateral plane could be adjusted for various wind conditions. J. Porter Shaw Collection. (Courtesy San Francisco Maritime Museum.)

Chinese shrimpers at work close inshore .... The north shore of San Pablo Bay and Hunter's Point were favorite grounds for shrimp. In 1957, China Camp, near McNear's Landing, was still the center of the shrimp industry in the bay area. (Courtesy San Francisco Maritime Museum.)

An oyster camp off South San Francisco .... Captain John Stillwell Morgan formed the Morgan Oyster Co. in 1887 and built a number of houses on piles on tidelands between Point San Bruno and San Francisquito Creek. The schooner *Commodore* and sloop *Impossible* are at the far right with a barge next to them. San Francisco Bay cat boats are anchored off the buildings and Whitehall boats hang from davits. A number of barges containing oystermen are afloat beside the wharf about the middle of the picture. Clark Collection. (Courtesy Peabody Museum.)

Oystermen off the South San Francisco camp . . . . The schooner *Commodore* is at the left of the picture and the sloop *Imposible* in the center. Men are unloading oysters from the barges onto the wharf and packing them for shipment to San Francisco. Clark Collection. (Courtesy Peabody Museum.)

The oyster sloop *President* at anchor . . . . Built at San Francisco in 1891 and measuring 21 tons net, *President* belonged to the Morgan Oyster Co. and was used to carry oysters from the camps to San Francisco. Beyond her is a San Francisco Bay cat boat with sail set, and in the distance is a fence built to keep stingrays out of the oyster beds. (Courtesy San Francisco Maritime Museum.)

Soon after 1900, gasoline engines replaced sail for Italian fishermen . . . . By the time this picture was taken at Fishermen's Wharf in 1939, the transition was long-since accomplished. The close family relationship of these later boats to the feluccas, shown earlier, is clear. The flat-bottomed skiff at the far left is interesting. (Photo by Karl Kortum.)

The sardine fleet at Point San Pablo, 1948 . . . . There are 104 purse-seiners under way, at anchor, and moored alongside the reduction plants in this picture. At the end of the point, to the left, and also at the far right are six fish reduction ships. The purse-seiners shown had delivered 12,000 tons of sardines in the preceding 24-hour period. This was the last great year of the sardine industry in the San Francisco Bay region. Farther around the point, in the upper left corner, Captain Clark's yacht harbor can be seen, its breakwater formed by six steam schooners and a ferry boat, all dismantled. (Courtesy Parr-Richmond Terminal Co.)

PURSE SEINERS UNLOADING
SARDINES FOR THE MANUFACTU
OF FISH MEAL AND FISH OIL

PARR-RICHMOND TERMINAL No. 4
POINT SAN PABLO
RICHMOND, CALIFORNIA

Fishermen's Wharf in 1956 . . . . Now located at the foot of Taylor Street and stamped as a tourist attraction, the atmosphere has changed since the old days at Union Street. The boats shown are rigged with power "gurdys" for salmon trolling. By the use of such highly mechanized equipment, hand-lining is eliminated and the labor of taking salmon is considerably eased. A comparison with the 1939 photograph reveals considerable alteration in the design of the boats. (Courtesy Port of San Francisco.)

Chapter IX

Whaling and Deep-Sea Fishing

SAN FRANCISCO Bay served as a base for whaling, deep-sea fishing at long distances, and sealing, as well as for the local fishing dealt with in the previous chapter. Of these activities, the connections with whaling were the earliest and the longest continued. Whaling ships from the United States appeared in the Pacific in 1791, and after 1815 they were occasionally off the California coast. In 1826 Captain Frederick Beechey reported finding seven American whalers anchored in Richardson Bay taking on fresh water and firewood. The Hawaiian Islands were the chief rendezvous for whalers in the Pacific, however, and during the height of the Gold Rush whaling captains avoided San Francisco in order not to lose their crews. In the 'fifties they began to return, however, and in 1858 the Pacific Oil and Camphene Works was established there to process spermacetti and sperm oil. By 1857 there were ten vessels operating out of San Francisco in search of whales.

The inroads of petroleum competition and losses in the whaling fleet due to ice conditions and the Confederate cruiser *Shenandoah* damaged the whaling trade severely, but after 1865 the remaining whalers increasingly used San Francisco as a base, and between 1884 and 1892 over 40 ships a year operated from there. From 1885 until about 1905, San Francisco was the principal whaling port in the world, its wooden,

steam whalers bringing back profitable cargoes of oil and whalebone from the Arctic Ocean. In 1883 the Pacific Steam Whaling Co. was formed to bring together what had previously been competing groups, and the next year the Arctic Oil Works were established in the Potrero to refine, transport, and trade in whale oil. After 1908, the price of whalebone collapsed, and the last of the Pacific Steam Whaling Co. vessels were laid up in 1910.

Along the Pacific Coast, there was considerable hunting for grey whales, they were occasionally taken in San Francisco Bay itself, and the small steamers which were used in the business were often built and repaired there.

Another long-distance operation was codfishing in the waters of the Sea of Okhotsk and Bering Sea. Schooners began going north in this business in 1863, and sometimes as many as a dozen or fifteen schooners a year participated. There was some halibut fishing and salmon fishing by schooners operating out of San Francisco, but this was more generally done from bases in the north.

Sometimes whalers eked out a poor year by taking fur bearing animals, and in the latter years of the nineteenth century schooners went north especially to take fur seal. This trade from San Francisco, however, was less important than from British Columbia.

Whalers in Oakland Estuary about 1885 . . . . By the time this picture was taken, San Francisco Bay had become the world's chief whaling base. Vessels cruised in the Arctic Ocean and Bering Sea in the summer, and were laid up during the months that the whaling grounds were closed by ice. J. Porter Shaw Collection. (Courtesy San Francisco Maritime Museum.)

Three whaling barks in Oakland Estuary . . . . Like the last picture, this shows whalers laid up between seasons. Such a photograph as this seems as though it were more in keeping with New Bedford than San Francisco Bay. J. Porter Shaw Collection. (Courtesy San Francisco Maritime Museum.)

A Yankee whaler changes her hailing port . . . . *Gay Head,* built in New Bedford in 1877, had her registry shifted to San Francisco as a result of the migration of the center of activity of whaling to California. In this photograph, she is shown getting under way for a cruise to the Arctic. (Courtesy San Francisco Maritime Museum.)

Drying whalebone . . . . What appear to be palm fronds are actually pieces of whalebone as removed from the whale's jaw and put out to dry in the yard of the Pacific Steam Whaling Co. in the Potrero District of San Francisco. The San Francisco-built steam whaler *Orca* appears in the background at the left and, at the right, the merchant bark *J. D. Peters* is loading whale oil and bone to transport around the Horn to East Coast markets. Millen Griffith Collection. (Courtesy San Francisco Maritime Museum.)

The Arctic Oil Works in the Potrero . . . .
A lithograph by the Bosqui Engraving
and Printing Co. shows an unbelievably
neat industrial enterprise. Steam and
sailing whalers are shown moored at the
wharf and at anchor in the bay. With
increasing production of natural gas and
petroleum, whale oil declined in importance as an illuminant and a lubricant.
(Courtesy Robert B. Honeyman, Jr.)

Bowhead was the first steam whaler built
in San Francisco . . . . A 533-ton auxiliary
steamer with a compound engine, she
was completed early in 1882 by Dickie
Brothers for Charles Goodall. In this
picture, she is shown at anchor off Telegraph Hill with whalebone drying in
her shrouds. *Bowhead* was lost in the ice
pack in the summer of 1884. (Courtesy
Morton-Waters Co.)

A new steam whaler joins the fleet . . . .
Proudly flying the house flag of the
Pacific Steam Whaling Co. at the fore
and the National Ensign at the mizzen,
Narwhal puts to sea from San Francisco
on her first voyage. She was a wooden
auxiliary steamer built in 1883 by Dickie
Brothers measuring 524 tons gross. Remaining in the service of the Pacific
Steam Whaling Co. until the business
collapsed and she was laid up in 1910,
Narwhal had her engine removed and
served as a salmon packer, did a stint in
the movies, and went under the Mexican
flag in 1931. (Courtesy Morton-Waters
Co.)

The whaling industry of San Francisco Bay attracted boat builders from New Bedford . . . . With the transfer of the center of American whaling to the Pacific Coast in the 1880's, the New Bedford firm of J. C. Beetle moved its yard to Alameda. There they built whaleboats, as well as Whitehall boats and launches, for the Klondike trade in 1898. When whaling declined on the West Coast, the Beetle family returned to New England, where they continued to build small craft. J. Porter Shaw Collection. (Courtesy San Francisco Maritime Museum.)

The old whaling bark *California* . . . . Built in New Bedford in 1842, *California* had come to rest on the mud flats of San Francisco when this photograph was taken in 1909. (Courtesy Roy D. Graves.)

A steam whaler for the inshore business . . . .
Whaling close to the shores of California
did not require the large vessels of the
Arctic fishery. Here is the whale killer
Hawk in drydock on Oakland Estuary. The
whales that she killed would be brought
in to a coast whaling station for the taking
of oil and bone. David W. Dickie Collection. (Courtesy San Francisco Maritime
Museum.)

A San Francisco cod fisherman outfitting
for a season's work . . . . A deck view of
Louise, a typical bald-headed three-masted
schooner, built by H. Bendixsen at Fairhaven, California in 1892. She was the same
type of vessel as the schooner *C. A. Thayer.*
After years in the coastal lumber trade, she
was sold to the Union Fish Co. and fitted
for dory fishing after cod in Alaskan waters.
This photograph was taken in 1937, the
last year that she went north. Dories can be
seen nested forward, and large gasoline
tanks for the outboard motors of the dories
are in evidence on deck. (Courtesy San
Francisco Maritime Museum.)

Sealers were based at San Francisco . . . . This is the
three-masted schooner *Sophia Sutherland,* built in
1889 at Tacoma, which made a number of sealing
voyages to the north out of San Francisco. (Courtesy
San Francisco Maritime Museum.)

Chapter X

Useful Craft

As AT any other great port, the ships coming and going at San Francisco Bay were served by a variety of small craft. The tasks which they performed were not very different from those of similar vessels in other parts of the world, but their development and character nevertheless was an important part of the maritime history of the bay.

Before the Gold Rush had reached full tide, pilot boats were cruising off the Golden Gate to offer expert assistance to the masters of ships bringing passengers and cargo into the harbor. Frequent foggy weather and the swift tidal currents which ran in the Golden Gate, as well as within the harbor, made it the better part of wisdom to take a pilot even when regulations did not require it. At that, entering and leaving the port was often a dangerous business, and a good many ships came to grief on the rocks along the entrance. A bell boat was anchored off the harbor mouth in 1858 to replace the fog gun which previously had been fired at regular intervals from Point Bonita in thick weather. There has been a lightship stationed off the Golden Gate since 1898 to supplement the lighthouses on Point Bonita, Point Lobos and Alcatraz Island.

Tugs were at first cut-down steamers, but, by 1870, vessels especially designed for this service were being built at San Francisco. They were available to tow sailing vessels in and out of the harbor, desirable assistance in any but the most favorable weather conditions. Both steamers and sailing vessels found their aid important in coming alongside wharves and getting out into the stream along a waterfront where tides and currents made the management of a vessel at low speeds and in restricted waters especially troublesome. They also towed scows loaded with mud and rock dredged from channels and slips, moved barges loaded with cargo of all kinds, and maneuvered floats with freight cars aboard about the harbor. There were also big, seagoing tugs based at San Francisco which were available to tow a barge up the coast to Puget Sound or bring a log raft down from the Columbia, as well as serving for rescue and salvage work in emergencies.

With dozens of seagoing vessels often anchored in the harbor, a host of other and varied service craft were needed to wait on them. Whitehall boats carried men to and from the ships, doing duty similar to the steam and gasoline launches which were their successors in the business. Coal hulks and water barges brought fuel and water alongside vessels at anchor or supplemented loading from a pier. Fire fighting tugs and police launches were required as the life of the waterfront grew more complex. In the years before the bulkhead was completed, dredges were omnipresent and, afterward, they were frequently in use when a slip was being deepened or a pier was being reconstructed. These and other useful craft combined to keep coastwise and deep water vessels moving in and out of the harbor, and to provide for their needs while they were in port.

The pilot boat off the Golden Gate, 1855 . . . . This spirited drawing was made by Thomas A. Ayres and lithographed by Britton & Rey in San Francisco. At the extreme left is Point Bonita Light which was completed the year that this drawing was made. Point Lobos, surmounted by the outer telegraph station, is at the right. The clipper ship *Flying Cloud* is at the left of the pilot schooner, and is heading for the Golden Gate. At the right is the Pacific Mail steamer *John L. Stephens* arriving from Panama. The arrival of these two famous ships simultaneously makes an interesting picture although actually they never reached San Francisco on the same day. (Courtesy Old Print Shop.)

The San Francisco Bar Pilot schooner *Lady Mine* . . . . This handsome craft was built at Port Ludlow, Washington, in 1880, and measured 58 tons gross. (Courtesy Bowes and Andrews.)

Four San Francisco Bar pilots aboard the schooner *California* . . . . David W. Dickie Collection. (Courtesy San Francisco Maritime Museum.)

A rough day on the bar . ∴ . . The deck of the Bath-built pilot schooner *California* [II], formerly the yacht *Zodiak*. (Photo by A. F. Nelson.)

Taking the pilot under difficulties . . . . The San Francisco Bar can be a very nasty place indeed under certain conditions. Here is one of the Matson-Oceanic liners, either *Mariposa* [II] or *Monterey* [I] rolling deeply as she pauses to pick up a pilot on the way in from the Antipodes and Hawaii in the 1930's. Clark Collection. (Courtesy Peabody Museum.)

The pilot schooner *California* [II] greeting a new arrival . . . . This picture shows the Matson-Oceanic steamer Mariposa [III] arriving off San Francisco in October, 1956, on her way from the builder's yard in Portland, Oregon. (Courtesy Matson Lines.)

Goliah was twice a towboat . . . . Built by William H. Webb in New York in 1848, *Goliah* was the second American vessel built expressly as a tug. She came to California in 1851, and operated as a passenger steamer on the Sacramento River and the coast, undergoing reconstruction and enlargement in the process. In 1864, Captain Millen Griffith purchased her and placed her in service as a tug once more. This photograph, taken from Long Bridge, shows *Goliah* with her walking beam and big paddle-wheels behind a coasting schooner. In 1871 she was sold for service in Puget Sound where she operated until 1899. (Courtesy Society of California Pioneers.)

The first San Francisco-built tug . . . . *Water Witch* was a 40-ton tug built in 1866 for Goodall and Perkins, to tow their water barges alongside vessels at anchor in the bay. Here she is seen bustling past a downeaster with a scow schooner and a brigantine, both white-painted in the distance. From their water business, Goodall and Perkins developed into the major coastwise steamship operators. (Courtesy San Francisco Maritime Museum.)

The launch of the tug *Monarch*, 1875 . . . . James C. Cousins built this 195-ton tug for Millen Griffith at North Point. In the picture, taken just before *Monarch* was launched, Millen Griffith stands on top of the pilot house. In the background are two floating docks with a schooner and a barkentine in the one to the left and a schooner in the one to the right. There are three tugs present in the water, a British grain ship is anchored in the distance at the left, and a wooden vessel, probably a schooner, is under construction at the lower right next to the Dry Dock Exchange Bar. (Courtesy San Francisco Maritime Museum.)

The seagoing tug *Dauntless* . . . . A 144-ton vessel, *Dauntless* was built by the Risdon Iron Works in San Francisco in 1903. She was owned by J. D. Spreckels and Bros. Co. and later by the Ship Owners and Merchants Tug Boat Co. Behind her, the steam schooner *Excelsior* is coming in from the north with a deck load of lumber. William Muir Collection. (Courtesy San Francisco Maritime Museum.)

Red Stack; Black Stack . . . . Tugs of the Ship Owners and Merchants Tug Boat Co. formed what was known as the Red Stack Line, because of their crimson, black-topped funnels, while those of the Spreckels Tow Boat Co. made up the Black Stack fleet. In this photograph, towboats of both of the rival companies lie alongside a coal wharf at San Francisco. From left to right, they are: *Hercules* (Red Stack), *Dauntless* (Black Stack), *Sea Fox, Sea Rover, Sea Witch* (all Red Stack), and *Reliance* (Black Stack). (Courtesy San Francisco Maritime Museum.)

A San Francisco tugboat captain and chief . . . . Captain James Curley (right) and Chief Engineer Thorald Steen, of the Southern Pacific tug *Ajax,* which was built in Seattle in 1908. (Courtesy San Francisco Maritime Museum.)

Towing to sea . . . . The tug *Standard No. 1* gives a deep laden bark a good offing while her crew begins to set sails. Meeting sailing ships outside the Heads as well as towing them to sea was a major waterfront business in San Francisco for well over a half a century. Keen rivalry existed between owners, and the inbound shipmaster who had more than one tug within hail at a time was likely to get a good price. *Standard No. 1* was built at Oakland in 1913. William Muir Collection. (Courtesy San Francisco Maritime Museum.)

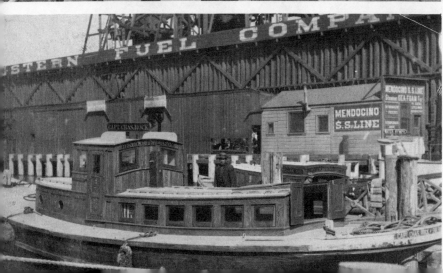

A successor of the Whitehall boats . . . . Henry C. Peterson, an important figure on the San Francisco waterfront, owned the launch *Capt. Chas. Rock* which is shown here alongside the bulkhead. He graduated from being an energetic Whitehall-boatman in the 'eighties to a prosperous launch and towing business during the early years of the twentieth century. The launch was named for a well-known commander of square-riggers who sailed out of San Francisco. She was fitted to put crews aboard ships in the stream and to provide general services. Beyond her may be seen the launch *Peterson No 1* and the tug *Water Nymph.* At the right is the office of the Mendocino S. S. Line which carried passengers as well as lumber in the wooden steam schooners *Sea Foam, Brooklyn,* and *Phoenix* between San Francisco, Point Arena, Little River, and Mendocino. The picture was taken in 1909. (Courtesy San Francisco Chronicle.)

A tug with a mud scow . . . . The tug *Pirate,* powered by a gasoline engine, was built as San Francisco in 1910. She is towing a scow carrying mud dredged from near the waterfront and to be dumped in a deep part of the bay. In the distance are Mission Rock and the Potrero District. (Courtesy San Francisco Maritime Museum.)

Tugs handled all kinds of ships . . . . The tug *Alert* moving the hulk of the former square-rigger *David Dollar* in San Francisco Bay. This picture was taken about 1929, when *David Dollar* (ex *Thielbek,* ex *Prince Robert*), which had been built in Liverpool in 1893, was abandoned. *Alert* was even older, having been built at Benicia in 1885. She was owned by the Ship Owners and Merchants Tug Boat Co. Notice the sad-looking figurehead of the old ship. (Courtesy San Francisco Maritime Museum.)

Tugs on the San Francisco waterfront in 1956 . . . . By the middle of the twentieth century, the Ship Owners and Merchants Tug Boat Co. had emerged as the major operator of bay and ocean going tugs on the Pacific Coast. This photograph shows the Red Stack tugs at Pier 25. (Courtesy Port of San Francisco.)

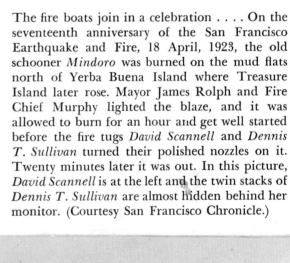

The fire boats join in a celebration . . . . On the seventeenth anniversary of the San Francisco Earthquake and Fire, 18 April, 1923, the old schooner *Mindoro* was burned on the mud flats north of Yerba Buena Island where Treasure Island later rose. Mayor James Rolph and Fire Chief Murphy lighted the blaze, and it was allowed to burn for an hour and get well started before the fire tugs *David Scannell* and *Dennis T. Sullivan* turned their polished nozzles on it. Twenty minutes later it was out. In this picture, *David Scannell* is at the left and the twin stacks of *Dennis T. Sullivan* are almost hidden behind her monitor. (Courtesy San Francisco Chronicle.)

The San Francisco Police Department's launch *Patrol* . . . . This may well have been taken on a trial trip. Certainly the officers amidships and in the stern look very smart indeed. Atlas Engine Co. Collection. (Courtesy San Francisco Maritime Museum.)

The salvage ship *Whitelaw* . . . . Thomas Irving Whitelaw was a Scot who jumped ship at San Francisco in 1866. After trying various waterfront jobs, he settled down in the salvaging business about 1875. This photograph shows his salvage steamer *Whitelaw,* a vessel of 176 tons which was built at San Francisco in 1882. Captain Whitelaw's wrecking yard on the waterfront was an amazing collection of marine junk. He died in 1932 at the age of 86. J. Porter Shaw Collection. (Courtesy San Francisco Maritime Museum.)

Chapter XI

Americans in the Cape Horn Trade

THE story of American sailing ships which plied from the Atlantic Coast to San Francisco and California in general around the Horn can be divided into three major periods. First, from 1822 until 1848, when the hide and tallow trade of the Mexican province was an attraction to a few shipowners; second, the years of the Gold Rush and on through the 1860's; and third, the long period from 1869 until the last of the sailing vessels in the business, about 1910.

The hide and tallow trade was one in which a small number of vessels, generally not more than a dozen in any one year, arrived on the California Coast from Boston, and began the exchange of their cargoes of all manner of manufactured goods for hides which would be made into shoes. It was not a vigorous business, but it served to establish bonds between California and the United States which were important in years to come.

With the end of the Mexican War, the cession of California to the United States, and the beginning of the gold excitement in 1848, a very active trade around the Horn sprang up. Many of the ships which came were ordinary merchantmen hastily fitted to carry passengers, and making the voyage in six months if they were fortunate. The demand for the speedy delivery of cargoes was such, however, that ships especially built and rigged for speed—the clippers—began to take the water along the Atlantic Coast and to engage in the California trade. *Flying Cloud, Sovereign of the Seas,* and *Young America* were three out of dozens of these magnificent ships. From San Francisco, they generally went in ballast to China and took cargoes thence to England or New York. Some of them came from the Orient back to San Francisco with passengers and cargo, however. By the 'sixties, the bloom was off the Cape Horn trade, and ships constructed for it were designed to carry more cargo and operate with smaller crews than the clippers. The name "clipper" stuck, however, and the lines of ships operated by Glidden and Williams, Sutton and Co., William T. Coleman, and others, some of them lasting down to the end of the century, were referred to as "clipper lines."

After the completion of the railroad across the continent in 1869, the Cape Horn trade was definitely confined to bulky, low-revenue commodities. United States Navigation Acts protected the business from foreign-flag competition, however, and hundreds of downeasters from the shipyards of Maine, sailed back and forth around the Horn until the end of the nineteenth century, and as late as 1909 there were still sailing ships in the business.

Brooklyn was a typical pre-Gold Rush trader . . . . In January, 1846, this 450-ton ship was chartered by a party of Mormons headed by Elder Samuel Brannan for a voyage from New York to California. She sailed on 4 February, with 238 passengers and a cargo which included three flour mills, a printing press, and a library of 179 volumes. Proceeding via Honolulu, she reached San Francisco at the end of July, just after the American "conquest". Her passengers and cargo landed, *Brooklyn* visited various coast ports and then sailed for Honolulu and Panama. (Courtesy M. H. de Young Memorial Museum.)

One of the great clippers at San Francisco . . . . *Sovereign of the Seas,* a masterpiece from the East Boston yard of Donald McKay, at the wharf below Telegraph Hill. Launched in June 1852, she was a ship of 2,421 tons, 258 feet in length, and with a beam of 44 feet. J. Porter Shaw Collection. (Courtesy San Francisco Maritime Museum.)

The clipper ship *Young America* alongside North Point Dock . . . . The Gold Rush created a tremendous demand for fast transportation to California. Merchantmen were pressed into service and eastern yards turned out new ships by the dozen, designed to reach San Francisco in record time. These were the celebrated clippers, and their spectacular sail-carrying, hard-driving skippers and resultant fast passages around the Horn drew world-wide attention. *Young America* was an outstanding example of the extreme clipper type and notable for her longevity. She was built by William H. Webb in New York. (Courtesy San Francisco Maritime Museum.)

124

A time of transition—California traders at Cowell's Wharf in 1868 . . . . This photograph shows a mingling of American full-rigged ships of like appearance, but actually reflecting a change in the composition of the Cape Horn fleet. After the Civil War, what few clippers remained from the '50's were giving way to the forerunners of the downeaster type. *Valparaiso* (in the right foreground, advertising her destination on a hoisted sail) and *Seminole* (next to the wharf, astern of her) were fast, handsome ships built in the early 1860's, but not quite sharp enough in hull form to be called medium clippers. *Sacramento* is probably the ship outboard of *Seminole*, and the clipper *Lookout* is on the left side of the wharf. In the distance at the left is the clipper *Midnight*, just arrived from sea, and at the right is *Gold Hunter* bending her foresail. This last was a Maine-built ship, precursor of dozens of downeasters which would be found in the trade for the next thirty years. Clark Collection. (Courtesy Peabody Museum.)

The Cape Horn trade held up for American square riggers until the end of the nineteenth century . . . . Ships built downeast for the trade, however, were designed with more of an eye to cargo capacity and economy of operation than were the clippers. *William H. Macy,* which is shown unloading at a San Francisco pier, was built in Rockport, Maine in 1883. At the time this picture was taken, she was owned by Eschen and Minor of San Francitsco, but she was still on the Cape Horn route. She ended her days in coastwise coal and lumber service. (Courtesy San Francisco Maritime Museum.)

The American ship *Great Admiral* sailing in through the Golden Gate . . . . This is one of a long series of splendid marine paintings by Charles Robert Patterson with San Francisco settings. *Great Admiral*, named for Admiral David G. Farragut, was built at Boston in 1869. Beside her, the picture shows a number of characteristic San Francisco types from the steam schooner at the left silhouetted against Fort Winfield Scott, past the square rigger towing out, the coasting schooner in the distance, and the tug, to two feluccas and one of the Oceanic steamers, either *Alameda* or *Mariposa*, at the right. (Courtesy Charles Robert Patterson.)

Courtesy Robert Patterson

The Cape Horners were greeted by a Whitehall boat . . . . *E. B. Sutton,* a Bath-built ship, completes her long voyage from New York and looks for an anchorage west of Goat Island. One of the first contacts the sea-weary crew will have with San Francisco is the Whitehall boat pulling up to the mizzen chains. In it will be a runner—a high pressure salesman, passing out cards to the captain and mates for a ship chandler or a hotel. Shortly, more boats will appear at the other end of the ship. The runners will entice the crew to this or that sailor's boarding house, bringing bottles of whiskey as evidence of their good faith. In a few weeks, when their wages are gone, the boarding-house masters will send the sailors to sea again, charging the ship's master so many dollars "blood money" for each man. William Muir Collection. (Courtesy San Francisco Maritime Museum.)

Sausalito: captain and mate put off to the ship . . . . The ship *Austria,* built at Bath, Maine in 1869, swings to her anchors in Richardson Bay, a favorite anchorage while awaiting the grain harvest. Her officers set sail to return to the ship, possibly after spending a day in San Francisco on ship's business and returning to Sausalito by ferry. Bortfeld Collection. (Courtesy San Francisco Maritime Museum.)

127

Llwellyn J. Morse shakes out her canvas to dry after a rain . . . . This photograph, taken after 1890, shows another downeaster which engaged in the Cape Horn trade. She was a ship of 1,393 tons, built at Brewer, Maine, in 1877. The characteristic elliptical stern of her type, a compromise between the earlier transom stern and the round stern which was introduced in the clippers and persisted in Bostonian and Canadian yards, is clearly shown here. At the right are the ferries *Thoroughfare* and *Ukiah*. Photo by Howard Tibbetts. (Courtesy San Francisco Maritime Museum.)

The career of the ship *Frank Jones* ended in the Golden Gate . . . . Built in New Hampshire in 1874, *Frank Jones* made only two round voyages between New York and San Francisco. On 30 June, 1877, the tug *Monarch* towed her out through the Gate bound for Manila in ballast. A fresh gale was blowing and the towing hawsers parted twice. Although both anchors were let go, the wooden full-rigger drifted onto the rocks and her bottom was badly holed. Futile attempts were made to get her off, but the fine vessel was eventually given up as a total loss and auctioned for $4,750. Fireman's Fund Collection. (Courtesy San Francisco Maritime Museum.)

On the decks of the downeaster *St. Paul* . . . . The mate, Robert Dunn, is the young man with the cigar; the second mate, Tom Williams, wears the dark shirt and galluses. When this picture was taken, the ship was in port at anchor with officers, petty officers, and relatives aboard, but no crew yet signed on. The setting is the fiferail at the foot of the "built-up" mainmast. By the time *St. Paul* was built at Bath in 1874, solid spars of a size for the lower mast of a 1,900-ton ship were difficult to find, and masts made of several sections banded together were common. The cast iron fly-wheels of the ship's "Liverpool pumps" can be seen abaft the mast. (Courtesy Andrew Nesdall.)

The last sailing ship to be hove down in San Francisco . . . . "Heaving down" was the ancient method of repairing a ship's bottom without using a dry dock. The vessel was internally strengthened to take the strain, her masts shored up with timbers, and then powerful tackles leading to horse-operated capstans on the wharf, pulled her over until the keel was exposed. Here is *Lucile,* hove down by the Havaside Co. alongside Union Street Wharf in 1901. A crew of caulkers then recaulked the bottom and renewed the copper sheathing. This sheathing, to keep marine borers out of the wooden bottom, was characteristic of the downeasters. *Lucile* was twenty-five years old when this work was done, having been built at Freeport, Maine, in 1874. Two portable coal hoppers may be seen on the left side of the wharf. H. T. Havaside Collection. (Courtesy San Francisco Maritime Museum.)

The bark *William P. Frye* standing in to the Golden Gate . . . . One of the last bids of the Maine yards for the continued economic survival of the big sailing ship was *William P. Frye,* a steel four-master, built by A. Sewall and Co., of Bath, in 1901. Her tonnage was 3,374 gross, and she was 332.4 feet long, 45.4 feet beam, and 26.2 feet in depth. William Muir Collection. (Courtesy San Francisco Maritime Museum.)

Alex Gibson loaded one of the last "New York general" cargoes for San Francisco.... When she sailed from New York on her last westward passage around Cape Horn on 1 July, 1900, there was no other ship on berth for San Francisco. This was unprecedented, and her departure virtually marked the end of the regular use of sailing ships on this route. *Alex Gibson* was built at Thomaston, Maine, in 1877, and engaged in the grain, lumber, and case oil trades as well as carrying general cargoes. After 1901, she was used mainly in the export lumber trade from Puget Sound, and in 1911 was converted to a coal barge. (Courtesy Andrew Nesdall.)

Deepwater aristocrats awaiting a rise in freights.... Four square-riggers, *Reuce, Abner Coburn, Henry Failing* and *Governor Robie* (left to right), are here seen in layup in Oakland Estuary during the first decade of the twentieth century. All four vessels were built in Maine in the early 1880's, and had successful careers in the Cape Horn trade to San Francisco and the case oil trade to the Orient and the East Indies. When this picture was taken, they were owned by the California Shipping Co., which had acquired the cream of the remaining American square-rigger fleet. Clark Collection. (Courtesy Peabody Museum.)

A steel downeaster discharges alongside a crowded pier.... The year is 1910. Standard Oil Co.'s big four-masted bark *Astral* has just arrived with general cargo from the Atlantic Coast. An up-to-date sailing ship, built in 1900, she has a fore-and-aft bridge running her length so that she can be worked when the main deck is awash in heavy seas. Sections of this bridge are hinged up out of the way so that cargo can be worked at the main and mizzen hatches. *Astral* was one of nine steel and three iron sailing ships built in the United States in contrast to several thousand built in Great Britain, France, and Germany. Farther out along the pier is a steamer, probably a British tramp, of the type which were crowding the square-riggers from the sea lanes. (Courtesy Society of California Pioneers.)

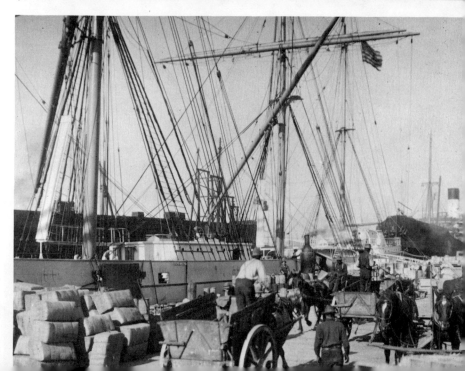

Chapter XII

Square-Riggers
Under Other Flags

THE second great era of trade in deep-water sailing ships to and from San Francisco was that of the last quarter of the nineteenth century centering in the grain trade and employing predominantly vessels under the British flag. From its almost entire dependence on outside sources for foodstuffs in the early days of the Gold Rush, Central California began to produce a surplus of grain for export by the middle 'fifties. In the years immediately following the Civil War, California wheat and barley production increased rapidly until by the 1880's 40,000,000 bushels of wheat annually were being raised. Most of this was exported, by sea. The growing wheat output in the plains states reduced the demand in the eastern United States, and a great part of the California wheat went to the European market. This trade gave California a valuable export commodity which it had previously lacked, and ships came bringing general cargoes or coal, loaded grain, and departed with their holds filled once more. In the peak year of the trade, 1880-1881, a total of 559 vessels loaded over 1,128,000 tons of wheat and barley and about 920,000 barrels of flour. These shipments were almost as large as the average annual exports of all dry cargo from San Francisco during the period 1925 to 1940. The wheat trade began to decline by 1890 due to changing

world demand, the resulting reduced prices, and soil depletion, and had virtually disappeared by 1910. Barley, although never exported in the quantity of wheat, continued to be an important item in the export statistics of San Francisco until World War II.

Since most of the grain went to foreign ports, and this trade was in no way protected by the Navigation Acts as was that between American ports, the greatest number of ships in the trade were British, mostly with iron or steel hulls. Of the 559 vessels in the 1881-1882 grain fleet, 345 were British, 149 were American, and the remaining 65 under other foreign flags including German, French, Norwegian, and Italian.

Most of the grain cargoes were consigned to Liverpool, which was the world's central market for them. During the months that the ship would be at sea between San Francisco and the English Channel, her cargo might be sold several times, and her master would pick up orders at Falmouth to discharge at Hamburg, Antwerp, Rotterdam, or London rather than Liverpool.

Although in reduced numbers, foreign square-riggers, including a large number of Frenchmen after 1900, due to a government subsidy for building and operating sailing vessels, continued to come and go through the Golden Gate carrying bulky cargoes until just after World War I.

British ships became common in San Francisco Bay in the 1870's .... California's growing grain export after the Civil War attracted iron ships, many of them medium clippers, to carry the harvest to the Liverpool market. The vessels shown here are *Duchess of Argyle* and *Carbet Castle*. Fireman's Fund Collection. (Courtesy San Francisco Maritime Museum.)

The iron bark *Golden Gate* loading grain at North Point .... At the left is a scow schooner, which has brought down a deck load of grain, which is being landed on the wharf preparatory to loading once more in *Golden Gate* for the voyage to Liverpool. The bark's mainsail has probably been loosed to dry after a rain, and seven men may be seen along the yard taking it in once more. (Courtesy Morton-Waters Co.)

The ship *Balclutha* loaded and ready to sail . . . . A steel ship built at Glasgow in 1886, *Balclutha* loaded grain in San Francisco Bay in 1887, 1888, 1889, 1896, and 1897. She was later engaged in the trans-Pacific lumber trade and, as *Star of Alaska,* was a cannery supply vessel for the Alaska Packers Assn. from 1902 to 1930. In 1954 she was purchased by the San Francisco Maritime Museum and restored insofar as possible to the state in which she took part in the Cape Horn trade. (Courtesy San Francisco Maritime Museum.)

British sailing ships waiting to load grain in Carquinez Strait, 1902 . . . . Although twenty years past the peak of the trade, 137 vessels cleared San Francisco Bay in the year 1902-3. This photograph, looking across the eastern end of the strait from Martinez to Benicia and into Suisun Bay, shows the four-masted barks *Dumferline, Dowan Hill, Reliance,* and other "limejuicers" awaiting the grain harvest so that they can go alongside the docks at Port Costa and take cargoes for the long Cape Horn voyage to Europe. (Courtesy Morton-Waters Co.)

Sausalito was another favorite anchorage while waiting for the grain harvest . . . . In the 1870's, the most characteristic square-rigger types trading to San Francisco were British iron ships and wooden downeasters of the same rig. The four American ships in the photograph are black painted; the British ships have the traditional row of mock gun ports painted on their iron hulls. The view is from the hill above Sausalito looking through Raccoon Strait with the Belvedere Peninsula on the left and Angel Island on the right. In years when freight rates to Europe were low, Richardson Bay and Carquinez Strait were more than seasonal anchorages for the grain ships. The four-masted bark *Buteshire* spent two years off Sausalito on one occasion, and the ship *Cawdor* lay at anchor four years off Martinez waiting for a rise in homeward grain freights. (Courtesy California Historical Society.)

Lady Isabella shakes out her sails to dry . . . . On a sunshiny morning after a night of rain, canvas blossomed the length of East St. and on ships in the stream—at least on those vessels with enough hands to man the buntlines and stow the sails once they were dry. The "brassbounders" (apprentice officers) in British ships were a blessing to the mate for such port duties. The men before the mast usually deserted on arrival at San Francisco where the business of luring them ashore and then shipping them on other vessels for so much "blood money" was highly organized. *Lady Isabella* was built at Dumbarton, Scotland, in 1882, and varied the usual pattern of British grain ships in that she was not port-painted. (Courtesy Morton-Waters Co.)

The crew of a "limejuicer" poses . . . . Officers and crew of the British ship *Derbyshire*, probably photographed upon the vessel's arrival in San Francisco and before the decimation of the crew by boarding-house runners. In addition to two dogs, the pony in the third row adds a surprising touch. Notice the low hatch-coamings, and the so-called "dolly winch", by which cargo was worked by hand. (Courtesy California Historical Society.)

Apprentices rowing in the bay . . . . While the grain ships awaited cargoes, their officers and apprentices sometimes found time passing slowly. Races between the pulling boats of the vessels were sometimes arranged, and this picture may show a practice for such an event. Three square riggers and a barkentine may be seen at anchor beside a survey steamer. A stern wheeler churns away toward San Pablo Bay and the rivers. (Courtesy San Francisco Maritime Museum.)

The battered *Willscott* arrives off the Golden Gate . . . . The British bark *Willscott,* on a passage from Kobe to British Columbia in 1898, was dismasted shortly after leaving the Japanese coast. The jury rig in the photograph was contrived, and she sailed nearly 4,000 miles in to San Francisco in 61 days. The vessel was rerigged at San Francisco, changed ownership, and passed under the Hawaiian flag. Dismasted again in 1901, she eventually became *Star of Iceland,* of the Alaska Packers Assn. (Courtesy San Francisco Maritime Museum.)

Loading grain from a barge at Oakland Long Wharf . . . . The French steel bark *General De Negrier*, 2,297 tons gross, built at Nantes in 1901, taking on sacked grain which has been brought down the river on the barge which is shown alongside. (Courtesy San Francisco Maritime Museum.)

French square-riggers became a common sight on the waterfront after the turn of the century . . . . Government shipbuilding and operating bounties for sailing vessels resulted in a great boom in French yards between 1897 and 1902. One of the ships so built, *Bayonne,* a full-rigger of 2,720 tons, is shown at Howard St. Wharf with her crew on stages painting over the bows. The French custom put the decorative "gun ports" along the bulwarks rather than along the sheer strakes as was the British practice. There are two coal hoppers in the middle of the picture, and the British *Beacon Rock* discharges at the left. Notice the small gas schooner unloading at the right with the help of a snatch block and horse power. Weidner Photo. (Courtesy San Francisco Maritime Museum.)

Beacon Rock loading salmon at Howard St. Wharf, about 1907 . . . . This photograph was taken the same day as the preceding one, but looks westward up the wharf toward East St. *Beacon Rock,* a steel square-rigger of 1,917 tons, with her home port at Glasgow, is loading canned salmon for the European market. The bow of *Bayonne* is visible at the left with the gas schooner beyond. The great two- and four-horse drays, used to move cargo to and from the wharves, are notable. In the distance, some of the sailor accommodations on East Street are visible with signs advertising "Jessie Moore Whiskey" and "California Steam Beer." Weidner Photo. (Courtesy San Francisco Maritime Museum.)

British square-riggers unloading coal from Newcastle . . . . Before the general use of oil for fuel on the Pacific Coast, vast quantities of coal were imported from the Pacific Northwest and Newcastle, New South Wales. The coal trade from Newcastle formed a convenient leg in the around-the-world voyages of the big British and French ships. They carried general cargo from Europe to Australia, coal from Australia to San Francisco, and grain from San Francisco around the Horn to Europe. In 1891 there were 107 arrivals in San Francisco with Newcastle coal, all sailing ships. This photograph was taken about 1908, when arrivals in the trade still numbered 56. Two big "limejuicers" are discharging on either side of the wharf, and the near vessel is down by the head, due to the coal taken out aft. In the foreground, a Navy steam launch tows a cutter toward man-of-war row. (Courtesy Morton-Waters Co.)

Barrelled cement, just arrived by sailing ship, is hauled into the city . . . . Coal and cement were two of the cargoes most frequently brought out around the Horn by European deep-water ships in the latter days of sail. Manufactured goods, wines, spirits, and beer frequently topped a cargo of barrelled cement stowed in the lower hold. Differing from later practice, open wharves still predominated in the early twentieth century. Windjammers, cargoes, donkey engines, drays, and draft horses formed a constantly changing picture for all to see. Weidner Photo. (Courtesy San Francisco Maritime Museum.)

Ship visiting in Carquinez Strait . . . . The scene is aboard a four-masted British bark waiting to load grain at one of the warehouses near Port Costa. Occasionally, when freight rates were low, ships waited half a year or more for a charter. The tedium of the long wait was relieved somewhat for those shipmasters who had their wives and families aboard by picnics ashore and social calls between ships. J. Porter Shaw Collection. (Courtesy San Francisco Maritime Museum.)

Chapter XIII

Sail in the Pacific Trades

A S SAN FRANCISCO became a center of commerce and finance, some of the capital accumulated there was invested in sailing vessels in the distant trades. The ships in the Cape Horn trade and in the grain trade were almost universally owned on the Atlantic Coast or abroad even though they might be individually under charter to San Francisco merchants. Local capital was represented in coastwise shipping almost from the start, and it found its way increasingly into deep-water shipping toward the end of the nineteenth century.

One direction which this investment took was in the ownership of vessels trading to Hawaii and the South Seas. A number of lines of Hawaiian sailing packets operated out of San Francisco from the middle of the nineteenth century until World War I. This business flourished especially after the Reciprocity Treaty of 1876 and the great influx of Hawaiian sugar to the United States. Both the Spreckels family and Captain William Matson operated both sailing vessels and steamers simultaneously for years, the former being dropped only when the cost of steamship operation became low enough to give them an economic advantage over sail in any type of trade.

Another type of shipping based at San Francisco was the support of Alaskan salmon canneries. Salmon fishing on the coast of Alaska became important about 1880. Because of the distance from a center of population, Alaskan salmon fishing and canning was done at shore stations operated seasonally. Fishermen, cannery workers, and equipment were sent north in the spring from San Francisco Bay, and at the end of the summer the men and the summer's catch were brought back once more. By the end of the 'eighties, a dozen or more firms were engaged in the business. Several independent operators joined forces in 1893 to form the Alaska Packers Association which came to send an average of thirty sailing vessels a year north from their base on Oakland Estuary. In 1912 they were operating fourteen canneries in Alaska and had a fleet of nine ships, one barkentine, eleven barks, three schooners, and sixty-two steamers—the last mainly small tenders. They sent vessels north under sail in 1929, and in 1930 *Star of Alaska* (formerly and again later *Balclutha*) made the voyage in tow of a steamer. By this time, steamships and diesel-engined vessels had taken the places of the sailing vessels. Beside the Alaska Packers, the North Alaska Salmon Co., Libby, McNeil and Libby, and other canning firms were in the business.

San Francisco capital also went into sailing vessels for general cargo trades. The transportation of Pacific Coast lumber to distant ports was one of the longest-lasting employments for such ships. Among the firms owning and operating such vessels—some of which were built for the business while others came into it from the Cape Horn trade—were Hind, Rolph and Co. and the Robert Dollar Co.

139

A Honolulu packet becalmed .... In 1880, Matthew Turner built the brigantines *Consuelo* and *John D. Spreckels* for the Hawaiian trade of John D. Spreckels and Brothers. At the same time that the firm acted as general agents for the Oceanic Steamship Co., they operated sailing vessels carrying sugar from the islands to San Francisco. This photograph shows *John D. Spreckels* with studding sails set. She was a wooden vessel of 267 tons and, like the others under the Spreckels house flag, she had a reputation for fast passages. (Courtesy Morton-Waters Co.)

Annie Johnson was a regular trader to Hawaii in the early 1900's .... William Matson, after commanding Spreckels ships, entered the business with his own vessels in the mid '80's. Here is Matson's iron bark *Annie Johnson*, formerly the British *Ada Iredale,* getting under way for Honolulu off the Golden Gate after dropping the pilot. Built in 1872, her tonnage was 1,049. The Matson Navigation Co. continued to operate sailing vessels in the Hawaiian trade until World War I, although it also had owned steamers from 1902 onward. Two other lines of sailing packets, the Hawaiian Line and the Planters Line, also engaged in the sugar business in the first part of the twentieth century. William Muir Collection. (Courtesy San Francisco Maritime Museum.)

In from Honolulu .... *Andrew Welch,* of the Planters Line, alongside her wharf in San Francisco. She was an iron bark built by Russell and Co. at Port Glasgow, Scotland, in 1888. Like the other Hawaiian packets, she was rather small, measuring only 903 tons, but, like them also, she was a smart and speedy vessel. (Courtesy San Francisco Maritime Museum.)

The barkentine *Makaweli* tries her sails for the first time . . . . The year is 1902, and the setting is just off the San Francisco Heads. *Makaweli*, freshly launched from the shipyard of W. A. Boole and Sons, Oakland. She was one of three handsome skysail-yard barkentines launched by Boole that year for the new firm of Hind, Rolph and Co. The other vessels were: *Koko Head* and *Puako. Mahaweli* was 194.1 feet long, had a beam of 39.5 feet and measured 899 tons gross. (Courtesy Morton-Waters Co.)

The schooner *Samar* engaged in distant trades . . . . She was a wooden four-master of 710 tons gross built by Hay and Wright, Alameda, for Saunders and Kirchmann, Inc. Built in 1901, she was taken to sea for the first time by Captain Marcus F. Asmussen who commanded her, with the exception of one voyage, for her entire twenty-year career. In December, 1921, he took her back into Oakland Estuary to lay her up on the mud flats off Government Island, her sailing career finished. In 1908, she brought a cargo of coal from Newcastle to San Francisco, and the next year she made a voyage to Cape Town with lumber via the Horn, and returned around the world. On one day of the homeward passage across the Pacific, she logged 340 miles. She came from Sydney to San Francisco in 46 days in 1916. (Courtesy San Francisco Maritime Museum.)

Captain Asmussen took his family to sea . . . . One of the conditions under which Captain Asmussen agreed to command Sanders and Kirchmann's new schooner *Samar,* was that he be allowed to take his wife to sea with him. At the insistence of the aggressive young Dane, the owners broke precedent, and Mrs. Asmussen sailed with her husband for twenty years. This photograph was taken on 14 February, 1907, when the Asmussens's daughter was christened. The captain leans on the wheel under its elaborately painted canvas cover, his wife sits in the center, and Irene Coulter, the baby's godmother sits at the left. The Asmussens's daughter is held by First Mate Alff Hansen. (Courtesy San Francisco Maritime Museum.)

The barkentine *City of Papeete* hove
down in the South Seas . . . . This San
Francisco vessel was one of a small
line of packets which operated during
the 1880's and 1890's to the Island of
Tahiti carrying general merchandise,
passengers and the mails. The usual
time consumed in making the round
trip was about three months. *City of
Papeete's* consorts in the trade were
the brigantine *Galilee* and the barkentine *Tropic Bird*. She was built by
H. Bendixsen at Fairhaven, California
in 1883, measured 390 tons gross and
was 145.6 feet long. In her later years,
she passed to the ownership of the
Alaska Codfish Co. An interesting
comparison may be made between
this incident of heaving down and
that of *Lucile* on page 129 (Courtesy
San Francisco Maritime Museum.)

Square-riggers in Oakland Estuary
awaiting the coming of spring, 1904
. . . . As the Cape Horn trade
dwindled, old ships gravitated to West
Coast ownership, and some found employment as tenders for salmon canneries in Alaska. The Alaska Packers
Assn. owned comparatively few ships
in the early years of the century, and
usually chartered at least half its fleet
for any season from the laid up ships
in the Estuary. The ship in the foreground is *Two Brothers*, built at
Farmington, Maine, in 1868. Albert
Gilberg Collection. (Courtesy San
Francisco Maritime Museum.)

Star of Holland starts her annual
voyage north . . . . By the beginning
of World War I, the Alaska Packers
Assn.'s "Star" fleet of iron and steel
sailing vessels was well established. As
the tug backs the bark out into Oakland Estuary, the decks are crowded
with fishermen and cannery hands—
soon to be separated into their separate living quarters, each with its own
galley and bill of fare. The "China
hold" occasionally became the resi-
dence of Oriental undesirables, and
during these trips it was presided over
by armed guards. William Muir Collection. (Courtesy San Francisco Maritime Museum.)

Preparing for a season of fishing in Alaska . . . . Coal being sacked and loaded aboard the tender *Alitak* at the Alameda yard of the Alaska Packers' Assn. This will be used in the donkey boilers of the ships and at the canneries. Beyond the pier lies *Star of France*. H. L. Cohen Photo. (Courtesy San Francisco Maritime Museum.)

An air view of the yard of the Alaska Packers Assn. at Alameda . . . . The ships lie along lightly built wharves in Fortman Basin with the buildings and machine shops of the yard at the right. Twenty square riggers, two schooners, two steamers, and four small steam tenders are visible. More vessels are laid up around Government Island and farther up the Estuary at the right. H. L. Cohen Photo. (Courtesy San Francisco Maritime Museum.)

By 1941, *Star of Finland* was the last square-rigger left in Oakland Estuary . . . . Alaska Packers, which had bought their first steamer in 1925, had not sent sailing ships north since 1930. The bark *Star of Finland* was built as *Kaiulani* by the Sewalls of Bath, in 1899. Astern of her lies the old Rolph tug *Storm King,* and across the wharf from her are the steam schooner *Celilo* and the tug *Henry J. Biddle.* The steam schooners laid up in the right foreground are: *Van-* *guard, Elizabeth, Santa Monica, Santa Barbara,* and *Wellesley.* In the distance are the Wilson Bros. steam schooners *Oregon, Idaho,* and *Svea.* By the end of 1941, rising freight rates occasioned by World War II had sent *Star of Finland* to South Africa with a cargo of lumber (under her original name), and *Storm King, Vanguard,* and *Elizabeth* had been sold for service in Central America and Mexico. (Photo by Karl Kortum.)

A schooner discharging barrels of salted salmon from Alaska . . . . These "salteries", or "salting stations", were simpler installations than the canneries, and required less capital. Usually a schooner, rather than a square-rigger, acted as tender. Notice the dray at the left, and the men loading barrels on it with dray stakes. J. Porter Shaw Collection. (Courtesy San Francisco Maritime Museum.)

Chapter XIV

Coastwise Ships

FROM what had been only one of four or five equally unimportant landings on the coast of California, San Francisco assumed a position of dominance as a result of the population increase which followed the discovery of gold. As the metropolis of the Pacific Coast, it was the economic hub of the whole region from San Diego to Alaska, and coastwise shipping services extended north and south from the Golden Gate. These existed to transport passengers, and to bring in needed goods as well as to distribute the products of San Francisco and the surrounding territory.

Trading ships had provided coastwise transportation in the years before 1848, but the requirements of the coastline in this regard had been easily satisfied. Even before the discovery of gold, plans were completed for the establishment of a steamship line from Panama to California and Oregon as a means of giving the Pacific Coast relatively fast and dependable connections with the rest of the United States. The Gold Rush made this steamship service an artery of the first importance, and the vessels of the Pacific Mail Steamship Co. and its competitors were the principal link between California and the Atlantic Coast until the completion of the transcontinental railroad in 1869.

Meanwhile, San Francisco's importance as an economic and social center led to the establish-ment of coastwise steamship lines to ports in California both north and south as well as to the Pacific Northwest. Even after the advent of rail connections with Southern California and Oregon, the coastwise steamers carried thousands of passengers each year to and from San Diego, Los Angeles, Portland, and Puget Sound. In addition, many small ports and landings had their only contacts with the outside through water connections until the coming of paved roads and motor transportation well on in the twentieth century.

Coastwise shipping served to bring to San Francisco the great quantities of timber from the forests to the northward which the growing city and its hinterland required. Sailing vessels, mostly schooners, and "steam schooners" shuttled back and forth between San Francisco and the lumber ports for nearly a century. Ships also carried the coal from the mines of Vancouver Island and Puget Sound which, despite its poor quality, was used in great quantities before the general adoption of oil as a fuel.

The coastwise trade north and south of San Francisco was heavily hit by the labor disturbances of the 1930's, and the resultant increased costs in the operation of ships. A combination of economic factors reduced coastwise maritime commerce very markedly in the twenty years after 1930.

Two old stagers at the Pacific Mail wharf, about 1873 . . . . The vessel at the right is *California,* built in 1848, and the inaugurator of the Panama to San Francisco service in 1849. When this picture was taken, she had been considerably rebuilt and was in the trade between San Francisco and San Diego. To the left of *California* is *Senator,* also a '49'er, having come from service on the Maine coast that year. She was first employed in the Sacramento River trade with great success, but from 1855 until 1882, she engaged in coasting voyages, mainly from San Francisco to San Diego. The two vessels dimly seen at the left have not been identified. J. Porter Shaw Collection. (Courtesy San Francisco Maritime Museum.)

The Panama trade called for big steamers . . . . This photograph shows *Golden City,* a wooden side-wheeler built in New York in 1862, at anchor in San Francisco Bay. She was 343 feet long, and measured 3,590 tons gross, which made her a very large ship for her day and type. These steamers were famed for their good food and comfortable accommodations, and they offered the fastest and easiest route between the Atlantic and Pacific coasts until the trans-continental railroad was finished in 1869.

Orizaba was long familiar on the California coast . . . . This steamer was built in 1854 for a line from New York to Mexico, but she was sent to the Pacific two years later and, after plying in the isthmian trade for nearly ten years, the California Steam Navigation Co. bought her in 1865. She passed through the hands of Holladay and Brenham, and the Pacific Mail and, in 1875, was purchased by Goodall, Nelson and Perkins. Under all these owners, she remained in the local coastwise trade, usually from San Francisco to San Diego, from 1865 until she was broken up in 1887. This spirited painting is the work of Joseph Lee, and is dated 1876. J. Porter Shaw Collection. (Courtesy San Francisco Maritime Museum.)

A coastwise flyer coming in from the south . . . . The Pacific Coast Steamship Co.'s *Santa Rosa,* the pride of the fleet in the 'eighties, approaching San Francisco past the old Cliff House and Seal Rocks. She was a standby of the San Francisco-San Diego express service from 1884 until her wreck, near Point Arguello, in 1911. *Santa Rosa* was 326.5 feet long, and measured 2,417 tons gross.

An incredible assembly of the Pacific Coast Steamship Co. fleet at San Francisco . . . . From left to right, the steamers are: *Alex Duncan, Coos Bay, State of California, Santa Rosa* and *Santa Cruz* (in right foreground). Another steamer, possibly *Queen*, lies behind *Santa Rosa* with only her foremast, part of her pilot house and her stack visible. A Whitehall boat hangs on the davits in the foreground. (Courtesy Norman R. and Ellen Longmore.)

Umatilla was a mainstay of the line to Puget Sound . . . . She was built as a coastwise collier in 1881, but had passenger accommodations added a few years later and, until the advent of new ships twenty years later, was kept regularly in the service from San Francisco to Victoria, Seattle and Tacoma by the Pacific Coast Steamship Co. In this picture, she is shown at the pier in San Francisco with her sails drying. On the wharf nearer the camera are two of the portable coal chutes into which the colliers discharged and which, in turn, directed the coal into dump carts. Clark Collection. (Courtesy Peabody Museum.)

A steamer of the "narrow gauge" . . . . *Bonita* was a good example of the small, general cargo and passenger carrier which operated both north and south of San Francisco, and provided contact with minor ports on open roadsteads which otherwise were out of touch with the rest of the world until the advent of paved highways, automobiles and trucks. She was a wooden steamer of 521 tons, built by Dickie Brothers in San Francisco, in 1881. Like almost all the coastwise liners of her day, she was owned by the Pacific Coast Steamship Co.

Governor represented a new era in coastwise transportation .... In 1907, the Pacific Coast Steamship Co. brought out *Governor,* which, with her sister-ship, *President,* and the later *Congress,* set a high standard of performance and comfort for passengers on the service from Seattle to San Diego via San Francisco and San Pedro. She was a steel vessel 392 feet long, of 5,250 tons gross. Originally her funnels were more conventional than those shown, but the extremely tall ones were fitted in order to improve the draft of her furnaces. She was lost in Puget Sound in 1921. (Courtesy San Francisco Maritime Museum.)

Overnight to Los Angeles .... *Yale* heading out the Golden Gate at about 4:20 in the afternoon; at 10 the next morning she would dock at Los Angeles Harbor. *Harvard* and *Yale* were built in 1907 for overnight service from Boston to New York around Cape Cod. They came to the Pacific in 1910, and entered the San Francisco-Los Angeles trade. Here they were highly successful and, after a period of service in the English Channel in World War I, they returned to the Pacific Coast. Between them they provided sailings between San Francisco and Los Angeles about four nights a week, as well as extending some trips to San Diego. *Harvard* was wrecked near Point Arguello in 1931, but *Yale* continued to operate until the collapse of the coastwise business in 1936. (Courtesy Morton-Waters Co.)

H. F. Alexander, San Francisco.

The high point of the coastal liners .... In 1915, James J. Hill placed the steamers *Great Northern* and *Northern Pacific* on the run between Flavel, Oregon, at the mouth of the Columbia River, and San Francisco on schedules which rivalled the Southern Pacific trains. After World War I, *Great Northern,* renamed *H. F. Alexander,* returned to the Pacific Coast and plied between Seattle, San Francisco and Los Angeles during the summer season from 1922 until 1936. She was 500 feet long, 8,357 tons gross and carried 585 passengers. Faster than *Harvard* and *Yale,* she was not an economical ship to operate, but was literally a pace-setter for the Pacific Steamship Co., successor to the Pacific Coast Steamship Co.

Schooners were the work-horses of the coasting trade . . . . This photograph dramatizes the large number of fore-and-aft craft passing through the Golden Gate in the age of sail. A trio of topmast three-masted schooners, one bald-headed three-masted schooner, and three two-masted schooners are all standing in to the entrance of the Bay, while a two-master heads the other way. Some idea of the prevalence of the schooner type on the coast is given by these figures: between 1850 and 1905, 182 two-masted schooners, 112 three-masted schooners, and 130 four-masted schooners (of over 100 tons) were built on the Pacific Coast. In the foreground of this picture are the ornate towers of Sutro's Baths and, in the distance, Point Bonita and Mount Tamalpais can be seen. (Courtesy Henry E. Huntington Library.)

The two-masted schooner *Bobolink* . . . . Built at Oakland in 1868, this 170-ton schooner represents the type of craft which was most numerous on the Pacific Coast for decades. She is a "one topmast schooner" such as originally ran to the Washington and Oregon ports, but, with the coming of the three-masters, her like concentrated on the "doghole" trade of the Mendocino coast. J. Porter Shaw Collection. (Courtesy San Francisco Maritime Museum.)

General Banning was an "outside port schooner" .... Built at the mouth of the Navarro River on the Mendocino County coast in 1883, she typified the best of the Pacific Coast two-masters. *General Banning* differed from the lumber schooners of the '60's and '70's in that these vessels were smaller and were usually "one topmast schooners"—a topmast was carried only on the main. She measured 177 tons gross. An "outside porter" loaded her lumber cargoes at exposed anchorages—outside ports—along the rugged coasts of Northern California, Oregon and Washington. Sonoma and Mendocino counties had many of these "dog holes" where a chute from the cliffs was used to get the lumber aboard, or the schooner loaded "under the wire" by means of an aerial tramway. It took consummate seamanship to get these little schooners in and out of these dangerous anchorages. This photograph shows *General Banning* winning the Master Mariners' race in San Francisco Bay on 4 July, 1884. Photo by Lowdon. J. Porter Shaw Collection. (Courtesy San Francisco Maritime Museum.)

A coastwise liner skipper .... Captain Thomas Reilly (left) was widely known as "Fog-Horn" Reilly because of his powerful voice. He was a colorful captain of steamers of the Pacific Coast Steamship Co. in the first part of the twentieth century. With him stands First Mate Lane, who was with Reilly on many steamers. Between them, it hardly seems that any situation could not be managed. This picture was taken aboard *Senator* [II] in 1908. (Courtesy Norman R. and Ellen Longmore.)

A three-master with a deck load
. . . . *Sadie* was a bald-headed
schooner of 310 tons gross, built by
Bendixsen at Fairhaven, California,
in 1890. In 1898, she achieved fame
by making a trip from San Pedro
to Gardner, Oregon, loading a
cargo of lumber and returning to
San Pedro in a few hours under
seventeen days. She made the south-
bound trip of over 900 miles in
about 80 hours. As a newspaper
said, "This is steamer time . . ."
William Muir Collection. (Courtesy
San Francisco Maritime Museum.)

C. A. Thayer discharging lumber
in San Francisco . . . . Known vari-
ously as Third Street Channel,
Channel Creek and Mission Creek,
the dredged inlet into what once
was Mission Bay was the site of the
hay wharf, the brick yards and the
lumber wharves. It was a favorite
haunt of the coastwise lumber
schooners, like *C. A. Thayer,* bringing their cargoes from Eureka,
Bandon, Coos Bay and Grays Harbor. *Thayer* was one of 35 similar
three-masted schooners built for the
lumber trade by Hans Bendixsen
at Fairhaven, on Humboldt Bay,
near Eureka. She was named for a
partner in the E. K. Wood Lumber
Co. Of all her sisters, *C. A. Thayer*
alone survived until 1956, when
she was purchased by the State of
California to be restored to her
original condition and preserved
as a symbol of what was once a
great maritime trade. (Courtesy
Allen Knight.)

Schooner towing out; fog coming in . . . . At Point Bonita, the fog horn operates an average of 858 hours a year, and yet photographs of the Bay Area with indications of fog are rare. The reason is obvious: fog conditions are not usually ideal for taking pictures. In this photograph, a three-master is being towed out of the harbor by a tug and, between her and the Marin shore of the Golden Gate, the fog is drifting in, as it does so frequently on a summer afternoon. The picture was taken from the Presidio and shows Fort Winfield Scott in the foreground. Photo by Charles R. Page. (Courtesy San Francisco Maritime Museum.)

A proud five-master ... . . The schooner *W. H. Marston* was built by W. F. Stone at San Francisco in 1901. She was rated at 1,169 tons gross and was the first five-masted schooner built on San Francisco Bay. This photograph shows her with flags at every masthead, sailing on her maiden voyage. Photo by Walter A. Scott. (Courtesy W. F. Stone and Son.)

A brigantine arrives with a deckload . . . . Shortened down to upper topsail, main skysail and spanker, this little coastwise trader is coming into San Francisco with a cargo of lumber from the north. Her port bower is ready to drop as soon as she reaches her anchorage and, with helm down, comes up into the wind. A few brigs and brigantines were built in the early days for the lumber trade for loading at Coos Bay, where the difficult entrance called for the superior handling qualities of a square-rigged vessel. Most of the 21 brigs and brigantines built on the Pacific Coast were for use on the Hawaii and Tahiti packet lines, or for inter-island service in the South Seas. (Courtesy San Francisco Maritime Museum.)

Schooners discharging lumber at the Pope and Talbot Yard . . . . Discharging lumber from a sailing vessel was a long and laborious process, usually taking several weeks and sometimes as long as a month. Here, longshoremen are putting the deckload of a schooner ashore, while, in the foreground, a tallyman keeps count of each piece. The vessel in the background, partly unloaded, is the bald-headed schooner *Okano-* *gan,* built for Pope and Talbot by Hall Bros., in 1895. She was 606 tons gross and generally carried about 800,000 feet of lumber, a good part of it on deck. The Third and Berry Street yard, shown here, regularly stocked seven million board feet of lumber, and was one of the largest in San Francisco. (Courtesy San Francisco Maritime Museum.)

The Channel was extensively used by the lumber fleet and scow schooners . . . . In this photograph, taken from the Fourth Street Bridge looking toward the bay, lumber schooners may be seen unloading at the right and scow schooners at the left. The three-masted schooner is *Sausalito,* built in 1903. In the distance is the Third Street Bridge. The picture was probably taken in the latter 1920's. (Courtesy Carl Christensen.)

The launch of the first steam schooner, 1884 . . . . Charles G. White launched *Surprise* on 18 October, 1884, from his yard at North Beach, San Francisco. The addition of steam power to the sail propulsion of the schooners was of great assistance in maneuvering in and out of the lumber loading "ports." Before long, the sails disappeared altogether, but the appellation "schooner" persisted until the last of the type had gone out of service. In the left center, beyond *Surprise's* stack, are the ruins of Meiggs Wharf. Farther to the right, the end of the seawall is visible with a big bark alongside. The retouching of the flags was done on the original photograph. (Courtesy San Francisco Maritime Museum.)

Schooner and steam schooner . . . . The transition from sail to steam in the coastal trade is symbolized by these two vessels photographed at North Point in 1905. The little *Westport,* in the foreground, was built by Boole at San Francisco, in 1888. She measured 211 tons gross and was one of the pioneers of her type. Astern of her, a two-masted sailing schooner is putting her cargo ashore. Sailing schooners were still common in 1905, although no new ones were built after that year until the World War I boom. *Westport* is discharging by swinging boom—sailing ship style. Later, a pair of stationary booms became standard steam schooner cargo gear. (Courtesy Society of California Pioneers.)

On a trial run, the owner and his family went along . . . . *Katherine's* hull was built in 1908 at Fairhaven, by Lindstrom, and then was towed to San Francisco for the installation of engines and boiler. It was common practice to tow engineless hulls to San Francisco from as far north as Oregon and Washington, and a cargo of lumber was thriftily brought down on the trip. *Katherine* is shown here on her trials in San Francisco Bay after engines had been installed. She is flag-bedecked and carries the emblem of her owner, the Redwood Lumber Co., on her stack. Her deckhouse is large enough to accommodate some passengers. (Courtesy Carl Christensen.)

Wapama was a big lumber schooner . . . . Her wooden hull, built at St. Helen's, Oregon in 1915, measured 951 tons gross, and she had a capacity of 1,050,000 board feet of lumber. There were accommodations for passengers in her superstructure at the stern. The picture of her unloading at the foot of Telegraph Hill was taken in 1931. She survived to be the last of her class as *Tongass*. (Photograph by John W. Procter.)

The steam schooner *Nehalem* unloading at San Francisco . . . . This vessel, built at Fairhaven in 1910, is a "three-island" type with bridge and engines amidships, rather than aft, as in *Katherine*. She would be known as a "double-ended" steam schooner, while *Katherine* was "single-ended." Notice the open construction of the midship section to permit the stowage of lumber on either side of the engine casing. Shipwrights are building a shelter on the wing of the bridge while a conference between the captain, representative of the shipwright firm, and boss carpenter goes on at the left. The engineer has just left this group and is walking toward the starboard side of the deck. David W. Dickie Collection. (Courtesy San Francisco Maritime Museum.)

Steam schooners unloading in Oakland . . . . In the foreground is the steamer *Svea* with the bow of another ship appearing at the left and a number of similar vessels on the Alameda shore in the distance. The location is approximately at the foot of Alice Street, Oakland. (Courtesy San Francisco Maritime Museum.)

Steam schooners were versatile . . . . Here is *Excelsior* taking passengers for Alaska on 28 July, 1897. She was the first vessel to leave San Francisco for Skagway and Dyea after the news of the rich gold discoveries in the Klondike had taken effect. She is alongside John Rosenfeld's Sons coal pier, and two of the movable chutes are clearly visible ahead of her. *Excelsior* was an 830 ton vessel, built at Eureka in 1893. J. Porter Shaw Collection. (Courtesy San Francisco Maritime Museum.)

A coastwise collier approaches her anchorage . . . . New England-built square-riggers were favorite vessels for the coal trade from British Columbia and Puget Sound ports to San Francisco. In the '70's and '80's, a number of downeasters were sold to San Francisco owners for this trade, and regular Cape Horners made a voyage or two between the Golden Gate and Cape Flattery, while awaiting a grain charter for Liverpool. Donald McKay's *Glory of the Seas* was a collier ship in the coastwise trade for seventeen years and the old clipper, *Dashing Wave*, had the reputation of being the fastest coal ship on the Pacific Coast. The photograph shows the bark *Gatherer*, built at Bath in 1874, and registering 1,509 tons. A four-masted lumber schooner is anchored off her bow and the steel "limejuicer" at the right is typical of the coal carriers from San Francisco's other source of supply: Newcastle, N.S.W. (Courtesy Morton-Waters Co.)

Kate Davenport as a coal drougher . . . . This 1,249-ton wooden ship was built at Bath in 1866. By the mid-1880's, she had shifted to Pacific Coast ownership and was in the coal trade. In the photograph she is shown lying at Green Street Wharf just south of the old Fishermen's Wharf. (Courtesy San Francisco Maritime Museum.)

Unloading coal for the Pacific Mail . . . . Although the portable coal hoppers shown elsewhere were common on the San Francisco waterfront, there were also piers designed especially for handling fuel. This photograph shows the Pacific Mail's coal wharf with a ship unloading into hand carts on rails which could be dumped into the company's storage bins. In the left foreground is one of the small wooden barks which were to be found on the Pacific Coast well into the 1880's. Clark Collection. (Courtesy Peabody Museum.)

Chapter XV

Deep-Water Steamers

SAN FRANCISCO became a great port at about the same time that the steamship became economically and mechanically suitable for long, trans-oceanic routes. Nevertheless, the great distances of the Pacific and the sparse population around much of its shoreline delayed the advent of regular steamship lines. When they did appear, San Francisco was their focus on the Pacific Coast until nearly the end of the nineteenth century when ports of the Pacific Northwest assumed an important role.

Trans-Pacific steamship lines were the first to be established. Such lines were proposed before 1850, but the first to go into operation was that of the Pacific Mail Steamship Co. from San Francisco to Yokohama and Hong Kong in 1867. The trade was not lucrative enough to draw much competition, but steamers under the Japanese flag entered it in 1898, and continued to be active contenders with American vessels. In addition to the operators of large passenger liners—Pacific Mail, Occidental and Oriental, Toyo Kisen Kaisha, Nippon Yusen Kaisha, Dollar Steamship Lines, and American President Lines—the twentieth century witnessed lines of freighters, mainly under the American and Japanese flags, in the trade as well.

An extension of the service to the Orient was the line around the world which the Pacific Mail pioneered in 1920, and which the Dollar Co. and the American President Lines later carried on.

Steamships began to ply regularly to Hawaii in 1866, but no line established itself firmly in the field until the advent of the Oceanic Steamship Co., founded by the Spreckels family in 1882. Leadership in this trade was assumed by the Matson Navigation Co. after World War I.

The Hawaiian trade was something of a springboard for a service through to New Zealand and Australia. Such a line was established in 1870, but met less financial success than the trade to the Orient. Under various auspices, American, Australian, and New Zealand, it was continued, the Oceanic Steamship Co. proving to be the longest-lived participant.

Intercoastal steamship service was inaugurated by the American-Hawaiian Steamship Co. via the Strait of Magellan in 1900. The opening of the Panama Canal in 1914 resulted in an intercoastal shipping boom which reached major proportions in the 1920's and 1930's, but suffered seriously from adverse rate factors and economic conditions thereafter. Not only were passenger and cargo liners operated between California and New York, but also from the Pacific Coast directly to Europe. This latter phase of the trade continued to flourish after the domestic intercoastal trade had fallen upon evil days.

Tramp steamers, operating on no set schedule but taking cargoes wherever they were offered, began to invade the long, bulk-cargo routes which had been the preserve of the sailing ship, about 1890. They were frequent visitors to San Francisco Bay in the coal and grain trades until 1914, and they returned in smaller numbers after World War I.

159

The first trans-Pacific liners were wooden side-wheelers . . . . Here is the Pacific Mail steamer *Japan* coaling at the company's wharf at the foot of First Street, San Francisco, for the voyage to Yokohama and Hong Kong. She, with her sister-ships, *Great Republic, China* and *America,* was 360 feet long and measured 4,352 tons gross. Notice the wide-flaring "guards" built out to enclose the paddle wheels; her hull was 50 feet wide, but on deck she measured 79 feet. *Japan* entered service in 1868 and burned at sea off the China coast six years later. Clark Collection. (Courtesy Peabody Museum.)

Alameda was built for the Honolulu trade . . . . The Oceanic Steamship Co. went to the Cramp Yard at Philadelphia for *Alameda* and *Mariposa,* 3,100 ton iron steamers. Built in 1883, the ships ran to Australia for years, and *Alameda* enjoyed a long old age on the Alaska route, finally being destroyed by fire at Seattle in 1931. This picture shows her alongside the wharf in San Francisco with the bow of the bark *Alden Besse* at the far right. (Courtesy Carl Christensen.)

Steamers for the Sandwich Islands and the Orient off San Francisco . . . . The vessel under tow is *Australia,* of the Oceanic Steamship Co., which was a standby in the Honolulu trade for many years. To the left is *City of Peking,* an iron, screw steamer built by the Pacific Mail in 1874, which made 116 round trips from San Francisco to Hong Kong. She was the biggest Pacific Mail steamer for fifteen years, with a tonnage of 5,080. Behind her rises Yerba Buena Island. This picture was probably taken about 1890. (Courtesy Gilbert H. Kneiss.)

A White Star liner in San Francisco . . . . The Central Pacific and Union Pacific Railroads organized their own trans-Pacific line, the Occidental and Oriental Steamship Co., which went into operation in 1875. They chartered British steamers of the White Star Line, and their aim was to have leverage to influence the Pacific Mail to operate in their interests. Here is the steamer *Belgic* [II] sailing from San Francisco for Japan and China about 1890. Clark Collection. (Courtesy Peabody Museum.)

The Pacific Mail replaced the wooden paddlers with vessels of iron and steel . . . . Fashions in trans-Pacific liners changed little for twenty years after the company began to replace the wooden steamers with ships with metal hulls and screw propulsion. This photograph shows *Peru,* built by the Union Iron Works in 1892, at her San Francisco pier. She was 336 feet long and 3,528 tons gross, a smaller vessel than the Pacific Mail had been building a quarter of a century before. *Peru* remained in trans-Pacific and later, coastwise service, for the company until 1919. (Courtesy Henry E. Huntington Library.)

Japan's first bid for the trans-Pacific record . . . . The Toya Kisen Kaisha steamer *America Maru,* a steel vessel of 6,307 tons, is shown here departing from San Francisco for the Orient. She, with her two sisterships, *Nippon Maru* and *Hong Kong Maru,* inaugurated trans-Pacific passenger and express freight service to San Francisco under the Japanese flag. They were handsome ships with their clipper bows, white hulls and well-proportioned buff and black stacks. (Courtesy Morton-Waters Co.)

Texan sails for New York by way of the Strait of Magellan . . . . One of the big American-Hawaiian freighters getting under way from San Francisco in 1904 for the long voyage around South America. At the left, one of the Oceanic Steamship Co. vessels may be seen backing out of her berth bound for Honolulu or Tahiti and, to her right, a river steamer churns along. Angel Island is in the background. Square-riggers, the type of ship which *Texan* was driving from the seas, lie anchored in the distance. Gilberg Collection. (Courtesy San Francisco Maritime Museum.)

Tramp steamers usurped the place of many of the big square-riggers in the bulk trades . . . . The steamer *Belle of Spain,* shown in this picture, was a steel, single-screw steamer built at Newcastle, England in 1908. Dozens of other freighters like her frequented San Francisco Bay from the latter years of the nineteenth century until the First World War. (Courtesy San Francisco Maritime Museum.)

One of the Pacific Mail liners in from the Orient . . . . In the late 1890's, the Pacific Mail began to modernize its fleet and the construction of *Manchuria* and *Mongolia,* in 1903 and 1904, completed this program. They were 600-foot steel steamers of 13,638 tons gross and, when completed, were the largest vessels yet built in the United States. Here one of them is shown at anchor in Quarantine off Alcatraz Island. The pilot schooner *Adventuress* is in the foreground. (Courtesy San Francisco Chronicle.)

The Matson Line specialized in the Hawaiian trade from the beginning . . . . To free the midship section for cargo, the Matson Navigation Co. built a number of steamers with their engines aft. This was the line's characteristic type until the 1920's. Here is the first steamer *Lurline,* a 5,928 ton sugar and general cargo carrier built in 1908. She had limited passenger accommodations under the bridge amidships. (Courtesy Morton-Waters Co.)

The opening of the Panama Canal brought new trade to San Francisco . . . . In 1928, the Panama Pacific Line completed the first of three 20,000 ton turbo-electric passenger and cargo liners for the trade from New York to San Francisco. This vessel, *California,* is shown here coming into her berth at San Francisco on her maiden voyage. William Muir Collection. (Courtesy San Francisco Maritime Museum.)

Two Dollar liners at Hunter's Point, 1932 . . . . After World War I, the Dollar Steamship Co. assumed an increasingly important position in the steamship trade to the Orient and around the world. At the right is the 535-type steamer *President McKinley,* one of a large class designed for transports in World War I by the United States Shipping Board but completed after the end of hostilities. The Dollar Co. chartered and later purchased ten of these ships for their services. *President Coolidge,* the two-stacked steamer on the left, was built for the Dollar Co. about a year before this picture was taken. A 22,000 ton vessel, she and her sister-ship *President Hoover* were the largest steamers in trans-Pacific service from San Francisco before World War II. (Courtesy Bethlehem Steel Co., Shipbuilding Division.)

The Golden Gate has always been a hazardous place for navigators . . . . Fogs and strong tides, the latter reinforced by currents from the rivers of the interior, have combined to bring many a ship to grief in the entrance to San Francisco Bay. This picture shows the Gulf Pacific Mail Line freighter *Point Lobos* which struck a rock in a heavy fog on 22 June, 1939 and was beached on a sandy shelf outside Lime Point. It was possible to make temporary repairs and pull the ship off so that she eventually returned to service, but the picture stands for dozens of vessels both sail and steam which were not so fortunate. (Courtesy San Francisco Chronicle.)

A wreck in the Farallones . . . . The Liberty-type freighter *Henry Bergh,* doing duty as a troop transport, was wrecked in the Farallone Islands when homeward bound from the western Pacific at the end of May, 1944. (Official U. S. Navy Photograph.)

Matson's *Lurline* [II] heading out the Golden Gate for Honolulu . . . . This photograph shows the steamer, which was built in 1932, after her extensive reconstruction which followed World War II. In the background are Alcatraz Island and Fort Winfield Scott framed beneath the spans of the Golden Gate Bridge. (Courtesy Matson Lines.)

The first new trans-Pacific liners after World War II were *President Cleveland* and *President Wilson* of American President Lines . . . . In these ships, passenger accommodations were built into hulls which had been designed for high-speed troop transports. In this photograph, *President Cleveland,* just in from the Orient, is hove to off Alcatraz Island to take on health and immigration officers. (Courtesy American President Lines.)

A post-World War II cargo liner . . . . The Matson freighter *Hawaiian Builder,* a C-3 type vessel, steaming along the San Francisco waterfront toward her pier just south of the San Francisco-Oakland Bay Bridge. Yerba Buena Islnad appears beyond the fore part of the ship and Treasure Island may be seen astern of her. Although this vessel is a Hawaiian trader carrying assorted dry cargo westbound and mainly bulk sugar, molasses and pineapples eastbound, she belongs to a type found in many services. (Courtesy Matson Lines)

Night on the waterfront . . . . The 7,630-ton motorship *Arita Maru* of the Nippon Yusen Kaisha moored at her San Francisco pier in 1956. (Courtesy Port of San Francisco.)

Chapter XVI

The Navy in the Bay

THE same natural characteristics which made San Francisco Bay the center of merchant shipping on the Pacific Coast until the end of the nineteenth century recommended it as a naval base. Wide, protected waters for anchorages and extensive shorelines for the construction of docks made it attractive to the naval officers who viewed it from the very time of its discovery.

In the Spanish and Mexican periods of its history, San Francisco received visits from naval vessels under the American, British, and French flags, as well as from occasional Spanish warships. When the United States acquired California in 1846, the officers of the squadron of American men-of-war on the coast at once made plans for the establishment of base facilities on San Francisco Bay. Mare Island, lying between San Pablo Bay and the Napa River, at the western end of Carquinez Strait, was reserved for government use in 1850, and was purchased for a navy yard three years later.

At Mare Island, facilities for the repair and later the construction of ships were built and assembled. During and after World War I, the yard built the battleship *California,* as well as cruisers, destroyers, and submarines. When World War II made of San Francisco the major supporting base for the naval war in the Pacific, a host of new naval establishments at Hunter's Point, San Bruno, Treasure Island, Port Chicago, and elsewhere were acquired and developed.

During over a century in which San Francisco Bay has been an established naval base, it has never been under direct attack or witnessed a naval engagement. Scores of warships, American and foreign, singly, in squadrons, and in fleets, have visited the bay however, and have been provisioned, repaired, and trained there.

In addition to the comings and goings of vessels of the Navy, San Francisco has been a base for vessels of the United States Revenue Marine or Coast Guard. It has served as the assembly port for transports which, under naval escort, carried troops to the Philippines in 1898 and the years immediately following, and to the Western Pacific in immensely greater numbers in World War II. The bay is the home of the California Maritime Academy, a state-supported institution for training merchant marine officers, generally under the command of a retired senior officer of the Navy, and closely integrated with the national defense aspect of marine affairs.

The Navy Yard was established at Mare Island in 1854 . . . . This drawing of Mare Island was made by J. B. Dunlap at the end of 1855. Looking westward from Vallejo across the Napa River, it shows the yard and, beyond it, San Pablo Bay with Mount Tamalpais in the distance. The chief object of interest is the newly-completed floating dock at the left. It had been built in New York, shipped around the Horn in sec- tions, and had just been reassembled and placed in service. In the dock is the razee frigate *Independence*. The topsail schooner at the right and the felucca a little farther to the left, as well as the steamboat coming down the river from Napa and the ferry con- necting Mare Island with Vallejo, are also notable. The lithograph was printed by Britton & Rey, San Francisco. (U. S. Navy Official Photograph.)

Admiral Popoff brought a Russian squadron to the Bay in 1863 . . . . Because of their holdings in Alaska and Siberia, the Russians maintained a naval force in the Pacific. They lacked dry docks at their own bases and, therefore, the St. Petersburg government arranged for the Colonial Squadron to come to Mare Island for overhaul and repairs. In this drawing, only four of the five vessels of the squadron are shown. They are, from left to right, *Abreck* in the dry dock, *Rynda*, Admiral A. A. Popoff's flagship *Bogatyre* and *Kalevala*. The buildings of the yard appear dimly in the background. Work was completed on the ships in the spring of 1864, but the last of them did not leave San Francisco Bay until August of that year. (U. S. Navy Official Photograph.)

Mare Island was a quiet place in the years after the Civil War . . . . This photograph was taken in 1870 from Mare Island looking southward along the Napa River toward the entrance to Carquinez Strait at the far right. On the farther shore is Vallejo, with South Vallejo in the distance toward the right. The bay shown between them has long since been filled. Two steam sloops-of-war lie at anchor in the stream and a third is moored at the pier in the foreground. At the rickety wharf to the right of her is the old *Independence,* housed over and serving as a receiving ship. Beyond her is a steamer and, still farther to the right, can be seen the Bishop's Derrick, the yard's chief piece of lifting equipment. The sectional floating dock is beyond the derrick. A scow schooner lies off it in the river. (U. S. Navy Official Photograph.)

One of the Old Navy in the Napa River . . . . The wooden sloop of war *Pensacola,* 22 guns, at anchor off Vallejo. She was fitted with a telescoping smoke-stack and, in this photograph, it is lowered and, therefore, barely visible. (Courtesy Morton-Waters Co.)

The longest-lived naval tenant of the Bay .... The old *Independence,* built as a ship-of-the-line and later cut down to a frigate, was in the Pacific Squadron in 1847-1849 when California was taken by American forces, and came back to the coast in 1855 to stay. By 1861, she was serving as a barracks and receiving ship and she continued to do such duty until finally decommissioned in 1912. Here is *Independence* in the graving dock at Hunter's Point, doubtless receiving needed repairs in the early 1880's before the dock at Mare Island was ready for use. The additions and excrescences, which had been added to the old ship to make her more habitable or useful in her prosaic duties, are clearly visible. William Muir Collection. (Courtesy San Francisco Maritime Museum.)

A San Francisco product on speed trials .... The Union Iron Works built the monitor *Monterey,* and she is shown here running her trials in the Bay in 1893. Even in calm and protected waters, she was a very wet ship, but, in 1898, she crossed the Pacific to Manila safely and under her own power. In the background is Yerba Buena Island. David W. Dickie Collection. (Courtesy San Francisco Maritime Museum.)

The turn of the century brought new ship types . . . . In the foreground is *Pike,* one of the first American submarines in the Pacific. Built by the Union Iron Works, she and her sister, *Grampus,* were commissioned at Mare Island on 28 May, 1903. Two torpedo-boat destroyers are moored farther down the quay, outboard of the ex-hospital ship *Solace,* which served as their tender. Another former hospital ship, *Comfort,* is in the stream. The picture was probably taken about 1904, and looks northward up the quiet channel of the Napa River. (U. S. Navy Official Photograph.)

From World War I onward, Mare Island built large warships . . . . The 10,000-ton heavy cruiser *San Francisco* was launched in March, 1933, and is shown here at her outfitting berth in October of that year. She later returned to Mare Island for extensive repairs after her action in the Battle of Guadalcanal. (Courtesy National Archives.)

The waterfront of Mare Island in 1952 . . . . In the foreground at the right are machine shops with building ways and dry docks beyond them. The picture looks southward toward Carquinez Strait and the bridge can be seen at the far left. (U. S. Navy Official Photograph.)

Hunter's Point in 1941 . . . . When the Navy purchased the Hunter's Point dry docks from the Bethlehem Steel Co. in 1940, they left them under Bethlehem's operation on a lease agreement until after the outbreak of war with Japan. This photograph, taken in June, 1941, shows a machine shop under construction next to the two graving docks. The changes which took place at Hunter's Point in the next four years were phenomenal. (U. S. Navy Official Photograph.)

Hunter's Point in 1945 . . . . The Navy purchased the dry docks at Hunter's Point in 1940, and at once began extensive new construction. Most of the land shown in the left half of the picture was filled after 1941 and the new docks, shops and storage facilities were products of the war years. A comparison with the photographs of the Hunter's Point docks on pages 63 and 165 will show how great the change was. U. S. Naval Drydocks, Hunter's Point, were managed as an annex to the Navy Yard, Mare Island. (U. S. Navy Official Photograph.)

On 6 May, 1908, under lowering clouds, the Atlantic Fleet steamed through the Golden Gate . . . . This completed the first leg of the fleet's voyage around the world. It was the first really large collection of men-of-war to visit the bay, and the occasion aroused great public enthusiasm. Here, the line of pre-dreadnought battleships is led into the bay by *Connecticut*. Fort Winfield Scott appears at the far left, while Point Bonita and Lime Point may be discerned on the Marin shore of the Golden Gate. (Courtesy San Francisco Maritime Museum.)

A foreign visitor in a hurry . . . .
In the early weeks of World
War I, the Imperial German
cruiser *Leipzig* cruised off San
Francisco for nearly a week and
finally entered the harbor at 1
A.M. on 17 August, 1914. She
coaled, took on provisions, her
officers left valued personal ef-
fects in the keeping of Mayor
Rolph, and she sailed again at
midnight the same day, bound
on a cruise against British and
French shipping to the south.
Later, *Leipzig* joined the squadron of Admiral von Spee, took
part in the Battle of Coronel,
and was lost at the Battle of the
Falklands. This photograph,
taken in San Francisco Bay,
shows the ship on her brief visit
that August day in 1914. (Courtesy Randolph Brandt.)

Carriers coming into port, 1956
. . . . Two *Essex*-type aircraft
carriers of the First Fleet entering San Francisco Bay. The
Golden Gate Bridge is clearly
visible, and in the distance at
the left is Point Bonita. Sightseeing sailing yachts and power
craft are present in considerable
numbers. (U. S. Navy Official
Photograph.)

The Coast Guard cutter *Oliver
Wolcott* having her picture
taken . . . . This trim little
steamer was built at San Francisco in 1873. She measured 199
tons gross and carried two guns,
one of which points toward the
camera through the open port.
Officers and crew stand on deck
as though they are aware that
their ship is being photographed.
Four square-riggers lie at anchor
in the background. (Courtesy
Morton-Waters Co.)

The quarter deck of the Revenue Cutter *Bear* . . . . San Francisco Bay was *Bear's* operating base for forty years. She was built in Scotland as a sealer in 1874, was purchased by the Navy ten years later, and came to the Pacific under the flag of the Treasury Department in 1886. Until she was condemned and decommissioned in 1926, *Bear* cruised annually to Bering Sea. Then she became a marine museum for the city of Oakland, accompanied the Byrd Antarctic Expedition in 1933, and saw service in the Atlantic in World War II. (Courtesy San Francisco Maritime Museum.)

A veteran of Manila Bay anchored off Sausalito . . . . The Revenue Cutter *Hugh McCulloch,* which was in Dewey's squadron at the Battle of Manila Bay, is shown here in Richardson Bay on a quiet morning. A considerable washing hangs between her bowsprit and fore-yard. The San Francisco Yacht Club is at the left of the vessel, the ferry slip appears just to her right and, in the distance, are several grain ships at anchor awaiting cargoes. (Courtesy Randolph Brandt.)

A captured rum runner . . . . In the last days of Prohibition, Coast Guard Patrol Boat No. *256* took the 60-foot speed boat *Mizpah* together with 200 cases of just-landed liquor on 5 January, 1933 at Capitola, in Santa Cruz County. Here captor and prize are moored at the foot of Hyde Street the next day. In the center distance is the Customs tug and, at the left, is the Hyde Street ferry slip. (Courtesy San Francisco Chronicle.)

The California Maritime Academy . . . . First organized as the California State Nautical School in 1929, the state's maritime academy occupies a campus at the west entrance to Carquinez Strait. This photograph shows the classroom building, mess hall and gymnasium in the foreground, and the 7,000-ton training ship *Golden Bear* [II] is moored at the wharf at the right. In the distance is Carquinez Bridge, spanning the strait and, beyond it, are the buildings of the California and Hawaiian Sugar Refinery at Crockett. (Courtesy California Maritime Academy.)

Chapter XVII

Sport on the Bay

THE combination of the bay's great expanse of sheltered water and the presence in San Francisco and other towns of men who could afford pleasure craft led inevitably to the building and sailing of yachts. Although the shoal waters around much of the shore of the bay, the high winds which prevail from the westward especially during the summer months, and the strong tides and currents which run in parts of the bay reduce somewhat the attractions of these waters to pleasure sailors, yachting early became a popular sport.

Informal sailing clubs were succeeded by more permanent organizations. The San Francisco Yacht Club was incorporated in 1869, and the Pacific Yacht Club, an offshoot, came into existence ten years later. In 1886 the Corinthian Yacht Club was formed with a view to encouraging the sailing of smaller and less pretentious boats than had been favored by the older clubs. Other, often shorter lived clubs, appeared elsewhere around the bay.

One aspect of pleasure sailing on San Francisco Bay was the popularity of racing between craft which were normally workers rather than yachts.

The Boatmen's Protective Association staged a regatta for workboats on 4 July, 1867, and this became an annual event under the auspices of the Master Mariners' Benevolent Association which succeeded the other organization the next year. Coasting barkentines and schooners, scow schooners, and any other craft which wanted to race were welcome at the 4th of July events. Even yachts were permitted, although they frequently came off poorly in competition with the working craft. The regattas were sailed regularly and were extremely popular with spectators as well as participants from 1868 until 1877, and then occasionally, in 1879, 1884, 1885, and 1891, after which they ceased.

With the passing years, fashions in pleasure boats changed. Steam and naphtha launches were followed by gasoline-engined craft, but sailing yachts retained a large degree of popularity throughout. The advent of power boats, however, made possible the extensive use of the rivers and sloughs around the bay. Hunting and fishing as well as cruising and racing played their part in the activities of pleasure craft in the region of San Francisco Bay.

179

Preparation for racing . . . . A variety of sailing craft at anchor off Mission Rock on 3 July, 1876. Whether they were sailing a special race or were getting ready for the Master Mariners' Regatta, which would normally be sailed on the 4th, is not clear. Grain ships, mostly light but loaded in one or two instances, are at anchor and alongside the Mission Rock terminal. Although Mission Rock had been built over at this time, it was still nearly 100 feet from shore and was reached by ferry. (Courtesy Society of California Pioneers).

The International Boat Race, 19 April, 1884 . . . . This was a race of boats from ships in the harbor at the time. The cutter with junk sails in the foreground is especially interesting. At the left is a rowing boat which may well be the dinghy from a scow schooner. Taber Photograph. (Courtesy Bancroft Library.)

Second gun at Martinez . . . . Yachts and a scow schooner in Suisun Bay. The yawl in the middle distance represents a rig which was especially popular in San Francisco Bay in the 1880's. J. Porter Shaw Collection (Courtesy San Francisco Maritime Museum.)

A regatta without yachts . . . . The Master Mariners' Regatta of 4 July, 1884 found the deepwater barkentine *Makah* pitted against the scow schooner in the right foreground. In this beat to windward, the scow has some advantage over her larger rival. J. Porter Shaw Collection. (Courtesy San Francisco Maritime Museum.)

The first big yacht on the Bay . . . . *Casco,* owned by Dr. Samuel Merritt, of Oakland, probably achieved her principal fame when she was chartered by Robert Louis Stevenson for a cruise to the South Seas in 1888. In her last days she was a sealer based at Victoria, B. C.   J. Porter Shaw Collection. (Courtesy San Francisco Maritime Museum.)

Virginia and *Little Annie* . . . . The schooner yacht, *Virginia,* was built as *Cornelius O'Connor* at White's Boat Yard, San Francisco, in 1879. She was rechristened *Virginia* by her third owner, Edwin White Newhall. She remained a fast and famous yacht on the bay until she was retired from use in 1915. Her crew were distinguished by the vivid red shirts they wore. Here is *Virginia,* flying the burgee of the San Francisco Yacht Club, afoul of *Little Annie,* of the Corinthian Yacht Club, a group which favored smaller boats than the older organization. (Courtesy San Francisco Maritime Museum.)

Houseboats on the bay . . . This 1898 photograph shows a type which remains characteristic of many of the quiet waterfronts around the bay. It was taken from Belvedere looking through Raccoon Strait, with the Tiburon ferry slips on the left and Angel Island on the right. Of the two ferry steamers shown, *James M. Donahue* is at the left and *Tiburon* at the right. (Courtesy John W. Procter Collection.)

Chispa heading for Carquinez Strait . . . . Another famous yacht in the Bay was *Chispa*, designed by Matthew Turner and built for Isidor Gutte, long commodore of the San Francisco Yacht Club. She was built in 1887, and won first prize in the San Francisco Yacht Club race the day after her launching. The Bermudian (leg-of-mutton) mainsail was a San Francisco specialty due to the strong winds and large expanses of water of the region. In the distance, at the center of the picture, the South Vallejo steamboat wharf can be seen. J. Porter Shaw Collection. (Courtesy San Francisco Maritime Museum.)

Commodore Gutte and kindred spirits aboard *Chispa* . . . . On the glass plate, this photograph is titled: "Signing Articles, or Observations." The commodore (third from left) was a *bon vivant* whose hospitality was famous, and a considerable aura of tradition gathered about his boat. Gutte died in 1908 and, in 1917, *Chispa* was sold for service as a freighter on the Mexican coast. J. Porter Shaw Collection. (Courtesy San Francisco Maritime Museum.)

Five Whitehall boats in a "mosquito race" . . . . Even these utilitarian craft were raced in sport, on occasion. This picture is taken looking east from San Francisco with Yerba Buena Island in the left and center distance. J. Porter Shaw Collection. (Courtesy San Francisco Maritime Museum.)

Laid up for the winter . . . . The yawl *Lolita,* temporarily housed over, serving as a base for the Cardilia Club, a duck hunting group, in the Suisun Marshes in 1883. J. Porter Shaw Collection. (Courtesy San Francisco Maritime Museum.)

Three girls in a boat—homeward bound . . . . The three daughters of the lighthouse keeper at Goat Island (Yerba Buena) attended school in San Francisco, there being no school on the island. They made the trip to and from the city daily in their sloop, which is shown here in an original pen sketch by W. A. Coulter. It was later published in the San Francisco *Call.* (Courtesy Gerald MacMullen.)

"What have you got?" . . . . Hunters in the tules of the delta region. J. Porter Shaw Collection. (Courtesy San Francisco Maritime Museum.)

A gasoline-powered stern wheel launch on Oakland Estuary. (Courtesy San Francisco Maritime Museum.)

A holiday outing . . . . The steam launch *Belvedere* with a Fourth of July party aboard in Sessions Basin, Oakland Creek. The year was 1898. J. Porter Shaw Collection. (Courtesy San Francisco Maritime Museum.)

Fun on the Sacramento . . . . A launch race on the Sacramento River about 1912. From left to right, the boats are: *Louise, Martha Ann,* unidentified, *Jennie O.* and *Red Rover.* (Courtesy San Francisco Maritime Museum.)

Chapter XVIII

Conserving a Tradition

I T IS a truism that when institutions and ways of doing things are in general use, they are accepted as matters of course; when they begin to disappear or are threatened, people think about preserving them. Thus, during the early years of San Francisco's maritime greatness, the clippers, downeasters, and "limejuicers", as well as the scow schooners, the river steamboats, and the ferries, were accepted as permanent parts of the ordinary scheme of things. Suddenly, almost before men were aware of what was happening, the square-riggers were gone and trucks were replacing the bay freighters. Then the paintings, models, photographs, and log books which still remained suddenly assumed a new interest.

The concern for the past which these changes evoked did not come all at once. Great libraries of the region, such as the Bancroft Library and the State Library at Sacramento, had been collecting maritime books and records for decades. The M. H. de Young Memorial Museum had a marine collection before 1920, and the Golden Gate International Exposition of 1939-40 presented a maritime exhibition which was later moved to the Merchants Exchange in the city. Many individuals, seafarers and otherwise, invested time, patience, and money in bringing together materials on the maritime history of San Francisco Bay and the Pacific Coast.

Many of these activities came together in the founding of the San Francisco Maritime Museum Association just after World War II. The museum which was established at North Beach became a gathering place for much of the material which had previously been in private hands. Its public exhibitions emphasized the use of photographs and they were organized intelligently to illustrate the important phases of the maritime history of San Francisco Bay and the adjacent waters. Models and parts of ships were used to demonstrate significant points of marine practice of the past. Paintings, prints, and books were collected, but their importance was recognized as primarily in the field of research rather than for wholesale exhibition. In addition to the development of its shoreside museum, the Association purchased *Pacific Queen,* almost the last of the British grain fleet, and her restoration under its auspices illustrated the possibilities of cooperation among all parts of the San Francisco maritime community. When this work was completed, she was given her original name, *Balclutha,* and opened for public inspection. With the cooperation of the California State Division of Beaches and Parks, a coastwise sailing lumber schooner and a steam schooner were obtained and their restoration undertaken. In its plans to preserve significant vessels to illustrate the past, the Association has not lost sight of the importance of the maritime character of San Francisco Bay in the Twentieth century. Its efforts are not only directed toward preserving tangible evidence of a great past, but also it is awake to the importance of collecting and safeguarding materials which will illustrate the maritime history of the region as its development goes on.

Excitement at the Beach . . . . On 5 July, 1909, the sloop *Gjoa,* in which Captain Roald Amundsen had pioneered the successful negotiation of the Northwest Passage, was beached just south of the Cliff House. Later she was moved on rollers to Golden Gate Park for permanent exhibition. She was a gift to the city of San Francisco by Captain Amundsen on behalf of Norway. (Courtesy San Francisco Maritime Museum.)

San Francisco's first full-fledged maritime museum . . . . After World War II, the San Francisco Maritime Museum Assn. was established and opened its exhibitions in the unused Aquatic Park Casino. The photograph shows the entrance hall with the figurehead of *Star of Peru* at the left, and the beakhead of the schooner *Commerce* and anchor of the razee *Independence* in the center. In addition to parts of ships and models, the Museum has made extensive use of photographs to illustrate the history of the maritime development of San Francisco (Photo by Don Meacham.)

Balclutha restored . . . . In 1954, the San Francisco Maritime Museum Assn. purchased *Pacific Queen* (ex-*Star of Alaska,* ex-*Balclutha*). After great labors, she was brought to a good approximation of her condition when engaged in the grain trade. On 19 July, 1955, she was towed across the Bay from Oakland Estuary where she had been refitted, and was berthed at Pier 43, San Francisco. At the same time, she was rechristened *Balclutha* by Mrs. Inda Frances Dunn, who was born aboard her in 1899. She is now open to the public as a museum ship. (Photo by Karl Kortum.)

INDEX *

*Abbreviations for vessel types: (bkn.) Barkentine, (bgn.) Brigantine, (C.S.S.) Confederate States Ship, (m.v.) Motor Vessel, (scow schr.) Scow Schooner, (schr.) Schooner, (str.) Steamer, (str. ferry) Steamer Ferry, (U.S.S.) United States Ship.